NEW DIRECTIONS FOR YOUTH DEVELOPMENT

Theory
Practice
Research

winter | 2012

Adolescent Emotions
Development, Morality, and Adaptation

Tina Malti | *issue*
editor

Gil G. Noam
Editor-in-Chief

JOSSEY-BASS ™
An Imprint of
🕸 WILEY

Adolescent Emotions: Development, Morality, and Adaptation
Tina Malti (ed.)
New Directions for Youth Development, No. 136, Winter 2012
Gil G. Noam, Editor-in-Chief
This is a peer-reviewed journal.

Microfilm copies of issues and articles are available in 16mm and 35mm, as well as microfiche in 105mm, through University Microfilms Inc., 300 North Zeeb Road, Ann Arbor, MI 48106-1346.

New Directions for Youth Development is indexed in Academic Search (EBSCO), Academic Search Premier (EBSCO), Contents Pages in Education (T&F), Current Abstracts (EBSCO), Educational Research Abstracts Online (T&F), EMBASE/Excerpta Medica (Elsevier), ERIC Database (Education Resources Information Center), Index Medicus/MEDLINE/PubMed (NLM), MEDLINE/PubMed (NLM), SoclNDEX (EBSCO), Sociology of Education Abstracts (T&F), and Studies on Women & Gender Abstracts (T&F).

NEW DIRECTIONS FOR YOUTH DEVELOPMENT (ISSN 1533-8916, electronic ISSN 1537-5781) is part of the Jossey-Bass Psychology Series and is published quarterly by Wiley Subscription Services, Inc., A Wiley Company, at Jossey-Bass, One Montgomery Street, Suite 1200, San Francisco, CA 94104-4594. POSTMASTER: Send address changes to New Directions for Youth Development, Jossey-Bass, One Montgomery Street, Suite 1200, San Francisco, CA 94104-4594.

SUBSCRIPTIONS for individuals cost $89.00 for U.S./Canada/Mexico; $113.00 international. For institutions, agencies, and libraries, $298.00 U.S.; $338.00 Canada/Mexico; $372.00 international. Electronic only: $89 for individuals all regions; $298 for institutions all regions. Print and electronic: $98 for individuals in the U.S., Canada, and Mexico; $122 for individuals for the rest of the world; $343 for institutions in the U.S.; $383 for institutions in Canada and Mexico; $417 for institutions for the rest of the world. Prices subject to change. Refer to the order form that appears at the back of most volumes of this journal.

EDITORIAL CORRESPONDENCE should be sent to the Editor-in-Chief, Dr. Gil G. Noam, McLean Hospital, Harvard Medical School, 115 Mill Street, Belmont, MA 02478.

Cover photograph by © Elena Elisseeva/iStockphoto

www.josseybass.com

Contents

Editor's Notes

> True morality, like beauty, needs more than intellect. It
> includes a feeling of good will for others that is warmed
> by an inner fire.
>   E. W. Sinnott, *The Bridge of Life* (1966)

EMOTIONS SHAPE THE landscape of our social and moral lives.[1]
What we feel is likely to influence how we think about situations
involving fairness, justice, or social inclusion. Our emotions about
morally relevant events strongly depend on our experiences and
evaluations of the social world.[2] For example, experiencing exclusion from a peer group may evoke a variety of negative, challenging emotions in a young person, which may influence his or her
future thinking about these situations. Conversely, making decisions about moral issues, such as including a child who has a mental disability into a group activity for reasons of fairness and
empathy, may cause positive feelings in the self. In turn, these feelings may influence one's evaluations of future situations.[3] These
examples show that emotional experiences are necessarily intertwined with evaluations of morally relevant situations in multifaceted ways.[4]

Emotions may also help adolescents adapt to challenges that are
inherent in everyday moral conflicts. For example, the anticipation
of guilt feelings after one's own wrongdoing may restrict amoral or
aggressive behavior and motivate reparative behavior, such as an
apology.[5] Vice versa, the absence of such emotions may hinder fair
decision making or limit moral behavior.[6] For instance, focusing
exclusively on the positive feelings associated with personal benefit
may contribute to amoral decision making and lead an individual

to weigh strategic considerations and self-interest over moral concerns.[7] The anticipation of moral emotions, such as guilt feelings over wrongdoing or empathy for an individual who is suffering from the consequences of a transgression, is likely to relate to morally relevant behaviors. Still, this does not imply that such anticipation always leads to adaptive or positive outcomes. For example, an individual who feels intense guilt about real or imagined wrongdoing might be more prone to maladaptation, such as depression or social anxiety.[8]

Examining the complex interplay between emotions and reasoning in the context of moral conflict is important if we are to understand how young people resolve and adapt to the social and moral conflicts that inevitably occur in their everyday lives.

The articles in this volume aim to explain how emotional experiences influence young people's decision making, reasoning, and morally relevant behaviors.

What are the gaps in current research and thinking about adolescents' emotions and moral development? Recent models of adolescent development have acknowledged the role of emotions in adolescents' thoughts about fairness and morally relevant behavior.[9] However, integrative research is still scarce, and we know little about the subtleties involved in the relation between various emotional experiences and decision making regarding moral issues.

This volume brings together perspectives from developmental science, education, and clinical science to discuss new approaches to emotions, morality, and socially adaptive behavior in adolescence. The main aims are twofold. The first is to summarize the recent developmental science literature on moral emotions and moral reasoning, and emerge with a more complete picture of how these two parts of moral development may be integrated into a holistic view of adolescents' developing morality. The second is to identify novel approaches to the study of adolescents' emotions in morally-relevant contexts. In addition, this volume highlights the implications for educating moral and emotional development.

The first three articles focus on the role of emotions in adolescents' decision making and reasoning about morally relevant situations. They also show how adolescents integrate affect and cognition in these situations. Wainryb and Recchia begin this exploration by discussing a framework for capturing adolescents' emotional experiences in the context of morality and understanding how these sometimes turbulent or bewildering experiences inform, enrich, and change their thinking about what is right and wrong. In the second article, Malti, Ongley, Dys, and Colasante describe the variety of emotions that adolescents experience in situations involving moral transgressions and social exclusion. Using empirical data from Canada, they show that sympathy helps adolescents anticipate other morally relevant emotions, such as guilt feelings. Cooley, Elenbaas, and Killen emphasize in the third article the relevance of group dynamics for adolescents' moral and emotional development. They argue that, with the increasing salience of group membership in adolescence, weighing the consequences of resisting group norms becomes more important.

Taking the topic of emotions and morality one step further, the next three articles discuss emotions in relation to morally relevant behavior and adaptation. In the fourth article, Krettenauer describes links between moral emotion attributions and children's and adolescents' social behavior. The links exemplify different forms of adolescents' ability to make moral judgments and take responsibility for their actions. Carlo, McGinley, Davis, and Streit summarize research in the fifth article on the roles of guilt, shame, and sympathy in adolescents' morally relevant behaviors. Using data from the United States, they provide support for the role of guilt and sympathy in adolescents' prosocial behavior. In the sixth article, Arsenio, Preziosi, Silberstein, and Hamburger shift the focus to low-income, urban adolescents' perceptions regarding the fairness of American society and how these perceptions relate to their emotional experiences and actual behavior.

In the final article, Broderick and Jennings provide an approach to support emotion regulation and reduce maladaptive behavior in adolescents by focusing on emotional awareness and mindfulness. They conclude that mindfulness, as taught in universal prevention programs, is a promising tool to promote adolescents' emotional development and adaptive behavior.

Taken together, these articles provide new ways of thinking about the development of adolescents' emotions in situations involving fairness, social inclusion, and caring. They summarize links between emotions and morally relevant behaviors, such as prosocial behavior and antisocial behavior, while also providing discussion of how to educate adolescents' moral and emotional development. Understanding the complexities in the relationship of adolescents' emotions, evaluations, and behavior in morally relevant situations is an exciting area for future research and practice.

I thank all my colleagues who contributed to this volume, as well as Sophia F. Ongley, Ella Daniel, Sebastian P. Dys, Tyler Colasante, and the Laboratory for Social-Emotional Development and Intervention at the University of Toronto. Furthermore, I thank our funders, the Social Sciences and Humanities Research Council of Canada and the Connaught Fund.

Tina Malti
Editor

Notes

1. Nussbaum, M. (2001). *Upheavals of thought: The intelligence of the emotions.* Cambridge: Cambridge University Press.

2. Drummond, J. J. (2006). Respect as a moral emotion: A phenomenological approach. *Husserl Studies, 22,* 1–22.

3. Hoffman, M. L. (2000). *Empathy and moral development: Implications for caring and justice.* Cambridge: Cambridge University Press; Kristjánsson, K. (2010). *The self and its emotions.* Cambridge: Cambridge University Press.

4. Eisenberg, N. (1986). *Altruistic emotion, cognition, and behavior.* Mahwah, NJ: Erlbaum.

5. Tracy, J. L., Robins, R. W., & Tangney, J. (Eds.). (2007). *The self-conscious emotions: Theory and research.* New York, NY: Guilford Press; Malti, T., & Ongley, S. (in press). The development of moral emotions and moral reasoning. In M. Killen & J. Smetana (Eds.), *Handbook of moral development* (2nd ed.). New York, NY: Taylor & Francis.

6. Arsenio, W., Gold, J., & Adams, E. (2006). Children's conceptions and displays of moral emotions. In M. Killen & J. Smetana (Eds.), *Handbook of*

moral development (1st ed., pp. 581–610). Mahwah, NJ: Erlbaum; Malti, T., & Krettenauer, T. (2012). The relation of moral emotion attributions to pro- and antisocial behavior: A meta-analysis. *Child Development*. Advance online publication. doi: 10.1111/j.1467-8624.2012.01851.x

7. Gasser, L., & Keller, M. (2009). Are the competent the morally good? Perspective taking and moral motivation of children involved in bullying. *Social Development, 18,* 798–816.

8. Oakley, B., Knafo, A., Madhavan, G., & Wilson, D. S. (Eds.). (2011). *Pathological altruism.* New York, NY: Oxford University Press.

9. Malti & Ongley. (in press); Arsenio et al. (2006); Eisenberg, N. (2000). Emotion, regulation, and moral development. *Annual Review of Psychology, 51,* 665–697.

TINA MALTI *is an assistant professor of developmental and clinical child psychology at the University of Toronto. She also holds an affiliate scientist position at the Jacobs Center for Productive Youth Development in Switzerland.*

Executive Summary

Chapter One: Emotion and the moral lives of adolescents: Vagaries and complexities in the emotional experience of doing harm

Cecilia Wainryb, Holly E. Recchia

Far from being unthinking energies or irrational impulses that control or push people around, emotions are intricately connected to the way people perceive, understand, and think about the world. As such, emotions are also an inextricable part of people's moral lives. As people go about making moral judgments and decisions, they do not merely apply abstract principles in a detached manner. Their emotions—their loves and sympathies, angers and fears, grief and sadness, guilt and shame—are inseparable from how they make sense of and evaluate their own and others' actions, the way things are, and the ways things ought to be. While this is not to say that emotions have a privileged role in morality, it does mean that emotions cannot be reasonably sidelined from the study of people's moral lives. Thus, an important part of formulating a theory of moral development is to articulate a framework for capturing children's relevant emotional experiences in the context of morally laden events. Such a framework should also help us understand how these sometimes turbulent or bewildering experiences inform, enrich, and change children's thinking about what is right and wrong and about themselves as moral agents. This article considers the research on the relation between emotion and moral thinking,

NEW DIRECTIONS FOR YOUTH DEVELOPMENT, NO. 136, WINTER 2012 © WILEY PERIODICALS, INC.
Published online in Wiley Online Library (wileyonlinelibrary.com) • DOI: 10.1002/yd.20038

offers a perspective that aims to broaden and elaborate our understanding of the connections between emotion and morality in adolescence, and sets a new agenda for research on this topic.

Chapter Two: Adolescents' emotions and reasoning in contexts of moral conflict and social exclusion

Tina Malti, Sophia F. Ongley, Sebastian P. Dys, Tyler Colasante

This article explores how adolescents feel and think about contexts of moral conflict and social exclusion. We asked twelve-year-old adolescents how they would feel about intentionally harming another peer, omitting a prosocial duty, and excluding another peer. We then asked them to explain the reasoning behind their feelings and report on levels of sympathy. In all contexts, adolescents anticipated a variety of negative emotions for reasons of fairness and empathy. However, more feelings of guilt were reported in contexts of intentional harm than in other contexts. Adolescents with high levels of sympathy reported more guilt, for reasons of fairness and empathy, than adolescents with low levels of sympathy. These findings provide a window into adolescents' emotions and reasoning regarding moral and social issues.

Chapter Three: Moral judgments and emotions: Adolescents' evaluations in intergroup social exclusion contexts

Shelby Cooley, Laura Elenbaas, Melanie Killen

This article examines children's moral judgments and emotional evaluations in the context of social exclusion. As they age, children and adolescents face increasingly complex situations in which group membership and allegiance are in opposition with morally relevant decisions, such as the exclusion of an individual from a group. While adolescents are often characterized as being conformists to group norms, research demonstrates that their judgments about fairness, justice, and rights can supersede negative or exclusive norms espoused by groups. Additionally, young people's emotional evaluations of members who do not conform to a group norm are in concert with these fairness judgments. Implications for social and moral development will be discussed in the context of empirical findings.

Chapter Four: Linking moral emotion attributions with behavior: Why "(un)happy victimizers" and "(un)happy moralists" act the way they feel

Tobias Krettenauer

This article addresses the question of why the emotions children and adolescents anticipate in the context of hypothetical scenarios have been repeatedly found to predict actual (im)moral behavior. It argues that a common motivational account of this relationship is insufficient. Instead, three links are proposed that connect cognitive representations of emotional experiences related to future (im)moral actions with decision making and action. Accordingly, it is argued that moral emotion attributions can represent a dominant desire (link 1), outcome expectancies (link 2), or an emotional response to anticipated (in)consistencies of the self (link 3). These three links exemplify different forms of moral agency that emerge in the course of children's and adolescents' development.

Chapter Five: Behaving badly or goodly: Is it because I feel guilty, shameful, or sympathetic? Or is it a matter of what I think?

Gustavo Carlo, Meredith McGinley, Alexandra Davis, Cara Streit

The article provides a brief review of theory and research on the roles of guilt, shame, and sympathy in predicting moral behaviors.

Two models are presented and contrasted. The guilt-based model proposes that guilt and shame jointly predict prosocial and aggressive behaviors. In contrast, the sympathy-based model suggests that perspective taking and sympathy are linked to such behaviors. In both models, prosocial moral reasoning is proposed as a possible mediator in these relations. Results from a study of college students suggest support for both models. Moreover, there is evidence that prosocial moral reasoning mediates the relations between these moral emotions and moral behaviors. The implications for the need to incorporate moral emotions and cognitions into existing models of morality are discussed and emphasized.

Chapter Six: Adolescents' perceptions of institutional fairness: Relations with moral reasoning, emotions, and behavior

William F. Arsenio, Susanna Preziosi, Erica Silberstein, Benjamin Hamburger

This article addresses how low-income urban adolescents view the fairness of different aspects of American society, including how wealth is distributed, the nature of legal constraints, and overall social opportunities and legitimacy. This research emerged from efforts to understand the moral and emotional nature of some adolescents' aggressive tendencies. Recently it has become clearer that aggression can serve many purposes and that, for some adolescents, aggression is a coherent though problematic response to larger familial, neighborhood, and institutional forces. Consequently, the authors focus on the connections between low-income adolescents' perceptions of institutional and interpersonal fairness, certain aggressive tendencies, and related emotion judgments. At the same time, relatively little is known about how low-income adolescents as a group perceive the fairness of wealth distribution and other broad aspects of American society. Consequently, a second important goal is to examine these adolescents' normative beliefs about institutional fairness at a time of growing financial and educational inequalities in the United States.

Chapter Seven: Mindfulness for adolescents: A promising approach to supporting emotion regulation and preventing risky behavior

Patricia C. Broderick, Patricia A. Jennings

This article reviews the contextual and neuropsychological challenges of the adolescent period with particular attention to the role that universal prevention can play in moderating the harmful effects of stress. The centrality of emotion regulation skills to long-term health and wellness suggests their importance in prevention and intervention efforts for youth. Mindfulness has been shown to be an effective means of reducing stress and improving emotion balance in research with adults, although research on mindfulness with adolescents is limited. The authors present available data and describe one potentially effective program for adolescent mindfulness: Learning to BREATHE.

NEW DIRECTIONS FOR YOUTH DEVELOPMENT • DOI: 10.1002/yd

*This chapter addresses the diversity of adolescents'
emotional experiences following their own acts of
moral wrongdoing.*

1

Emotion and the moral lives of adolescents: Vagaries and complexities in the emotional experience of doing harm

Cecilia Wainryb, Holly E. Recchia

FAR FROM BEING unthinking energies or irrational impulses that
control or push people around, emotions are intricately connected
to the way people perceive, understand, and think about the
world.[1] As such, emotions are also an inextricable part of people's
moral lives. As people go about making moral judgments and decisions, they do not merely apply abstract principles in a detached
manner. Their emotions—their loves and sympathies, angers and
fears, grief and sadness, guilt and shame—are inseparable from
how they make sense of and evaluate their own and others' actions,
the way things are, and the ways things ought to be. Although this
is not to say that emotions have a privileged role in morality,
it does mean that emotions cannot be reasonably sidelined from
the study of people's actual moral lives. Thus, an important part
of formulating a theory of moral development is to articulate a

NEW DIRECTIONS FOR YOUTH DEVELOPMENT, NO. 136, WINTER 2012 © WILEY PERIODICALS, INC.
Published online in Wiley Online Library (wileyonlinelibrary.com) • DOI: 10.1002/yd.20035

framework for capturing children's relevant emotional experiences in the context of morally laden events and understanding how these sometimes turbulent or bewildering experiences inform, enrich, and change their thinking about what is right and wrong and about themselves as moral agents.

In this article, we first consider briefly the existing research on the relation between emotion and moral thinking. Next, we offer a perspective that aims to broaden and complicate our understanding of the connections between emotion and morality in adolescence and set a new agenda for research on this topic.

The typical affective consequences of moral transgressions

The centrality of feelings of empathy or sympathy towards the distress of victims of moral transgressions is woven into the fabric of vastly different theories of moral development.[2] There is also some empirical evidence that starting at a very young age, children recognize that victims feel sad or angry and that systematic difficulties recognizing others' emotions and systematic deficits in empathy (that is, in the capacity to be aroused by others' emotions) are strongly associated with psychopathology, aggression, and delinquency.[3] In spite of this, and even as the consensus about the importance of integrating emotion into the study of moral development continues to grow, research on these issues has been scarce and quite narrowly framed.[4] Very few studies have assessed the actual emotions that children display during sociomoral events or the meanings that they make of their own and others' emotions in the aftermath of such interactions.[5] Rather, the main focus of the research has been on children's expectancies of the typical affective consequences of sociomoral events.

The main idea behind this type of research, consistent with the broader literature on affect-event links, is that children remember the emotional consequences of morally laden interactions and in future situations rely on those generalized links for anticipating the potential emotional outcomes of diverse courses of action.[6] The emotion expectancies of moral transgressions are thus deemed important inasmuch as they are thought to inform children's subsequent moral judgments and behavior.[7]

The widely accepted, though somewhat unexamined, assumption of this research paradigm has been that the typical affective outcomes of moral transgressions are sadness or anger for the victim and guilt for the perpetrator. The lion's share of this research has dealt with very young children in an effort to parse a somewhat surprising finding. For although most children expect victims of moral transgressions to feel sad or angry, children under the age of five tend to expect that successful acts of victimization (for example, getting another child's toy, seizing a turn on a swing) will make the victimizer happy, and it is not until the age of seven or so that children recognize that perpetrators may feel guilt or a mixture of guilt and happiness.[8]

Studies using this method have generated important insights into the normative age-related shifts that characterize the emotion expectancies of children between the ages of four and ten. Because the affective expectancies considered normative are well established by middle childhood, the scant research involving adolescents has focused on assessing individual differences in affective expectancies and ascertaining the prospective effects these individual differences have on the moral decisions and behavior of young people. Overall this research has shown that deviations from the normative affective expectancy—in the form of adolescents who expect perpetrators of moral transgressions to feel happy—are associated with victimization, aggression, and delinquency.[9]

In this article, we suggest that in normative populations, and especially when dealing with adolescents, the examination of the relation between emotions and morality in terms of the typical affective expectancies of moral transgressions may be too rigid and may neglect some key considerations that frame how youth make sense of their own experiences of harm doing. To illustrate this, we rely on hundreds of narrative accounts drawn from a number of studies in which youths between the ages of fifteen and seventeen were asked, in individual interviews, to describe an instance when they themselves had caused hurt or distress to a peer, a friend, or a sibling.[10]

Adolescents' emotional experience in the context of their own wrongdoing

Even a cursory examination of the accounts of adolescents makes it evident that emotion talk is pervasive in the way they narrate their own moral transgressions. Given previous research, it may seem unsurprising that adolescents almost always speak of the distress the victims experience.[11] Nevertheless, what is noteworthy in the accounts here is that adolescents are speaking not about the distress caused by a hypothetical perpetrator to a hypothetical victim, but rather about the distress they themselves caused to a specific person they know well. As might also be expected from previous research, many of their accounts include references to their own negative emotions. Consider the following example (all names are pseudonyms, but everyone's gender is unchanged):

My brother used to be on this really competitive soccer team, and uh, and he worked really hard at it, like he'd drive down two hours a day and everything to get to practice. ... And they were in the championship and I went down and I saw the game and they played pretty poorly, I mean I'm just saying. It was a pretty demoralizing loss and the team was pretty upset. Anyways, so we were driving back, and then we go to this restaurant and so we're just eating and talking about the game. ... And I just say, "Like okay, wait, you guys were just worse than the other team. Just a fact. Can we stop talking about this?" And uhhh it really, really upset my brother, and to be honest it was really insensitive. It was pretty uh mean-spirited. And so actually my parents kind of made me apologize to him, but I felt like I should, and so, I, I apologized to him and I talked to him about it and we ended up making up so. (Tom)

Tom's account illustrates a common situation in which a teen notices that his or her actions upset another person, feels badly about it, and acts to repair the relationship. Tom makes it quite clear that although his parents made him apologize, the motivation to do so was internal, as he seemed to have recognized that his statements were insensitive and mean-spirited. Thus, this narrative serves as a good instantiation of the typical affective expectancies inasmuch as, following a transgression, the perpetrator notices the victim's distress and guilt ensues. Still, although one might read Tom's account as implying that his regret was a direct outcome of his brother's distressed reaction, other examples underscore that guilt is not merely a knee-jerk reaction to distress. Consider the following example:

I was hanging outside during lunch in the courtyard with a couple of my friends, and I made a joke, like um just a joke about a kid named Larry. He makes jokes about everybody, but if he's made a joke to him, then he takes it real personal. So ... I did a joke at him, and I kind of made him feel bad. ... When I said that, he heard it, he got down about it, and I was like "Well, you make fun of everybody else. Why can't anybody make fun of you?" He's like, "Well, dude, that's just going over the line," and I'm like, "Dude, you have been over the line too much!" and he kind of just took it personal like he normally does. (Frank)

In this rather typical "you can dish it out but you can't take it" event, Larry claims that Frank's joke hurt him, but Frank rejects Larry's plight as unreasonable and unjust, even as he recognizes that "I kind of made him feel bad." Previous research shows that even preschoolers distinguish between legitimate hurt complaints and the complaints of "crybabies" and judge the latter to be spurious.[12] Evidence that neither children nor adolescents take another's expression of distress at face value suggests that guilt is not likely to be a simple automatic reaction to distress. Furthermore, it is also often the case that youths feel guilty about what they have done even in the absence of the victim's distress. Our narratives include many instances of teens who report feeling guilty about having excluded a friend or peer from an activity, even when—in their own telling—the person excluded did not display any overt signs of sadness or anger ("She just turned around and started talking to those other kids"). And adolescents also often report feeling guilty about having lied to or betrayed a friend, even when that person never found out about the lie or betrayal and therefore presumably never even experienced distress—for example, "Me and my friends were hanging out with some girls, and one of our friends called us and was like, 'Where are you guys?' and we were really close to his house … but we told him that we were at Henry's house and he's like, 'Oh, all the way out there.' … We were just lying, … I felt kind of bad."

Overall, these examples show that a guilt response is not merely a function of a victim's distress. For adolescents in particular, who are so attuned to the psychological landscape of their experiences, feelings of guilt often result from an evaluation of their own psychological states. Consider the following two examples:

My old friend Karen was like kind of nerdy, I guess you could say. Then I made a new friend, Diane. And like ever since then, I've always been like, quote unquote popular, you know. But me and Karen always had like, we always had that link, I guess you could say. And, but once I got to be friends with Diane, we would always make fun of her. Like not really like, "You're ugly," or whatever. Just like, "Why did you do that? That was dumb," or something. And, like at the time, I feel so bad that I did this, but at the time, like we just laughed about it and we thought it was funny. And then I, I was like thinking about it and I was like, "How could I do that to my former best friend," you know. 'Cause she was a person too and just 'cause I wanted to fit in with other people, I shouldn't have done that. So I like, this went on for a while. And after that I apologized to her and she accepted my apology, although I don't think I would have if someone would have done that to me. I would have been really hurt. And I found out that she cried all the time. And that just made me feel really bad that I did that. So ever since then, I don't make fun of people any more. (Linda)

Um, I remember the first time I punched Rita, I have no idea what we were in an argument about, but it was apparently really important at the time [laughing]. And we just got into a fight and whenever we got into a fight, we always just like walked away from each other and locked ourselves in our room, but I think she hit me first, and then I really hurt her, punching her, and I felt so bad after hurting her, like I was like crying, I was like, "I didn't mean to hurt you!" but she wouldn't talk to me, and I remember going to my parents' bathroom and locking myself in there so that they couldn't find me because I felt so bad. ... I remember she started crying, and that's when I felt really bad, cuz I didn't really mean to hurt her, but I was just so mad. (Nicole)

Though Linda took note of the hurt she caused to her friend and Nicole took note of the hurt she caused her sister, the accounts suggest that their experience of guilt was connected not merely to what they did or to how the other person responded, but to their evaluations of their own psychological state—Linda's callous intentions, Nicole's overwhelming feelings of rage. Similarly, in Tom's case, we might understand his regret to result not merely from his brother's upset reaction but from his realization that his own comments had been tactless. In each case, therefore, it appears to be the teens' appraisals and judgments of their own actions that gave rise and meaning to their sense of guilt or remorse. The fact that guilt is so intricately linked to the perpetrator's beliefs about herself or himself—who she is ("I wanted to fit in with other people") and who she strives to be ("How could I do that to my former best friend?")—is unsurprising given that guilt is a self-conscious emotion. It also explains why someone might feel guilty even when the "victim" does not express distress or is not aware of what happened. But this important fact is not often explicitly addressed in assessments of affect-event expectancies as measured using hypothetical stimuli, where it may seem as though guilt is the more or less direct or automatic outcome of doing harm or witnessing a victim's distress.

As indicated by their own accounts, teens' emotional responses in the aftermath of wrongdoing are also intimately connected to, and moderated by, their understandings and interpretations of relevant features of the events. In many cases, their appraisals of the facts and meanings of events give rise to a more mitigated sense of guilt or responsibility. Consider the following examples:

My best friend and I, I had invited him to come to the dance with me. And he's ... into fashion ... he's not feminine or anything but he likes to look good. And it was probably about five or six at night, and he came to my house, and it was dark outside, and he was wearing sunglasses. And I was like, "Why are you wearing sunglasses? It's dark and you're inside?" And I said it; there were two other people there. And I didn't think it would hurt his feelings. I was just like, "That's kind of odd." And then we were talking the next day and he's like, "Yeah, that wasn't really nice." And I was like, "I'm sorry. I didn't mean to hurt your feelings. I was just curious about that, 'cause not many people wear sunglasses inside at night." ... But he was just like, "Yeah, sometimes you say things that you don't really think about. I know they're not meant to intentionally hurt me, but sometimes they do." And so I'm like, "Well, okay I'll watch out for that." (Hope)

I remember him taking some of like my stuff, and so I was upset and so then I'd like take one of his games or something. And then throughout the day ... he'd like trip or something, and I'd be like, "Oh Henry, you're so clumsy." And then he'd say something: "Oh Patty you're so stupid." ... And then like at first it was just joking, and then it got more heated, so by the end of the day, we were pretty angry at each other. And so then ... we were getting ready for bed, I don't even remember what I said. But I was like, "This will be such a good comeback," or something. So then I like said it to him after he had said something really mean to me, and it like really hurt my feelings. And so then after he was like, "Patty, I'm sick of you making fun of me all day." And I was like, "Well, Henry, you were making fun of me too." So we just walked away, and he went in bed, you know, and he was crying, and then I was crying in the bathroom. ... He was faking being asleep; I knew he wasn't ... so I walked over to Henry's bed, and I whispered in his ear, I'm like, "Henry, I'm really sorry about what happened. I didn't mean to hurt your feelings, you know, and I'm sorry that we've been fighting; it's supposed to be a fun time on our vacation, but I know it's my fault but also, it, we're both at fault." Because we had both been contributing to the arguments and I know that we can be better. And I was like, "I love you and I want to make this better and I hope that you'll forgive me." So then I just went to bed, and then the next morning it was okay. (Patty)

Me and my friends were going snowboarding one time, and another friend wanted to come, but he had never been snowboarding before, and we didn't really feel like teaching him or whatever so ... we just kinda blew him off that day ... because we wanted to go and have fun and not teach him, like, how to do it. ... So I don't feel real good about leaving him there, but I don't know. It just seemed that we would have a lot more

NEW DIRECTIONS FOR YOUTH DEVELOPMENT • DOI: 10.1002/yd

fun if it was just us four … but having, you know, to hang out with this other kid and teach him all the stuff we already knew. … At the time it seemed like a good idea, … but now that I think about it, it wasn't that cool. … Once we blew him off and stuff, like … I didn't feel really cool. I felt like I was being a bad friend. (Duncan)

These accounts illustrate that adolescents might recognize, acknowledge, and regret the distress or hurt they caused in others, while at the same time considering other features of the situation that mitigate their sense of guilt. Hope regrets having hurt her friend's feelings and apologizes, and she even articulates what she has learned from the situation ("I'll watch out for that"), which will presumably guide her future actions. But she also construes the harm as unforeseeable—as the result of her friend's unanticipated misinterpretation of her own benign, or perhaps ambiguous, behavior ("And I didn't think it would hurt his feelings. I was just like, 'That's kind of odd.' … I was just curious about that, 'cause not many people wear sunglasses inside at night"). Patty too recognizes that her brother felt distressed, acknowledges her role in his feelings, and expresses regret about it; furthermore, she acts deliberately so as to repair the relationship. But all the while, Patty also constructs the situation in a way that conveys her unwavering belief that her brother shared in the responsibility for what had happened, that they were both at fault. And Duncan regrets having ditched a friend when he went snowboarding with his other peers, but also states that his motivation behind not inviting that friend along had been legitimate, or at least had seemed legitimate to him at the time. The fact that Duncan recognizes that wanting to enjoy himself is not an intrinsically harmful motivation—though one that, in his telling, ended up conflicting with being a good friend— ends up helping to mitigate his sense of guilt.

In these varied ways, all of these examples illuminate the processes whereby adolescents might account for their own wrongdoing and mitigate their sense of guilt (by way of construals that represent the harm as being unforeseeable, provoked, or motivated by incompatible though legitimate goals). While it is true that these types of construals may not always be necessarily factually accurate, they typically reflect what youths believe to have happened rather than being merely self-protective distortions or disengagement.[13] Importantly, it is worth noting that none of the narrators in the examples relies on these construals to undo the negative consequences of their harmful behavior or transform it into acceptable behavior. We return to this issue below.

Conclusion

The collection of narratives discussed above represents a far from exhaustive illustration of the ways in which emotions are implicated in teens' moral lives. Importantly, this review leaves out a slew of other emotions (affection and aversion, jealousy and resentment, pity and anger) that play a crucial role at various stages of teens' morally laden interactions. Nevertheless, the goal of the examples we presented was to show that the affective outcomes of moral transgressions may be more diverse and nuanced than expected and closely linked with adolescents' appraisals of fact and value. In fact, our examination of teens' accounts and sense making of their own emotional responding in the aftermath of harm-doing suggests several conclusions.

First, teens' own accounts underscore that guilt is not an internally unintelligent indicator—a bell that goes off upon causing or seeing suffering, forcing them to recognize the moral nature of a situation.[14] Guilt, like other emotions, is intertwined with and acquires its meaning from judgments of fact and of value. Implicit in the paradigm examining the typical emotional outcomes of moral transgressions is the expectation of a relation between the doing or noticing of distress and the experience of guilt. The examples reviewed above suggest that this relation is neither rigid nor automatic: it requires certain judgments and interpretations linking the two—and judgments and interpretations can vary widely. Thus, we suggest that discussions surrounding the typical affective expectancies of moral transgressions might benefit from exploring the interpretive processes that undergird youths' emotional responses.

But the examination of teens' own accounts of their moral transgressions also suggests that the common assumption that guilt is the most typical well-adjusted emotional outcome of moral wrongdoing may be predicated on an overly constricted view of what it means to be a moral person. While it is often taken for granted that being a moral person means doing good deeds and refraining from hurting others (and therefore that guilt serves to guide and support future attempts at avoiding wrongdoing), in the course of everyday social interactions, people of all ages inevitably act in ways that hurt or upset others. Sometimes they engage in behaviors while knowing (or suspecting) that their actions may harm or distress others because everyone's legitimate goals are bound to clash with those of others from time to time. People's actions can also result in unanticipated harm because misunderstandings and differences in interpretation are bound to occur in the course of normal interactions. Being a moral person therefore also entails grappling with and making sense of these experiences and reconciling the fact that one has hurt another person with the sense of oneself as imperfect but fundamentally a good and moral person.[15] Unmitigated feelings of guilt may not be warranted in all such situations and may also not be adaptive.[16] Guilt mitigated by an understanding of the complexity of social interactions and the inevitability of conflicts and misunderstandings may be conducive to grappling with one's wrongdoing in ways that facilitate repairing the injury, learning future-oriented lessons, and, importantly, constructing a mature and realistic sense of one's moral agency. Thus, our work suggests that it may be essential for research on the connections between emotional experience and moral judgment to recognize the complexity and variability of youths' morally laden experiences and consider how youths' patterns of sense making across different types of events may contribute in distinct ways to moral-developmental outcomes.

The work presented here also suggests that the absence of guilt is not necessarily the same as "happiness" or moral disengagement.[17] As shown in the narratives excerpts presented above and in previous work, in the aftermath of their own wrongdoing, youths are often able to maintain a complex perspective that includes a consideration of their own more or less justifiable motives and intentions and of mitigating circumstances, along with a concern for the victim's feelings and a sense of regret at having caused harm.[18] We propose that this more mitigated sense of guilt can be best understood not as moral disengagement but as indicative of the complexity of morally laden events—a complexity that teens are particularly good at recognizing. This ability to appreciate that they may have had some legitimate reasons for behaving the way they did while simultaneously remaining concerned about and engaged with the harm they caused to others suggests that youths' emotional experience in the midst of their own moral wrongdoing is considerably more complex than, and not likely to be captured by, the dichotomous expectancy of self-censure (in the form of guilt) or self-exoneration (in the form of happiness or a disregard for the victim's feelings). And while teens' complex accounts do not in any way contradict or invalidate individual differences findings related to adolescents who do attribute to perpetrators (or to themselves in the hypothetical role of perpetrators) positive emotions, they do suggest that at the very least, in the larger normative population, absence of guilt should not be seen as necessarily predictive of moral maladjustment.

Altogether, our work suggests that to understand the role of emotions in moral life, we may need an approach to conceptualizing the relation between emotions and morality that allows variation within individuals and flexibility across situations. Just as the exclusive absence of guilt would surely be maladaptive, we suggest that feeling overwhelming guilt every time one inflicts harm is also likely to be maladaptive. Our analysis suggests a different pattern of what may be healthy—one characterized by flexibility and recognition of the unique features and dynamics of different events and relationships. It also suggests the need for a different, more flexible research paradigm. Rather than assessing emotional experiences solely in the context of prototypical moral events implicating deliberate harm, it may be necessary to examine teens' responses to a variety of morally laden events. And rather than viewing variation solely in terms of individual differences (such that deviations from the typical affective expectancy are thought to spell trouble), it may be important to examine individuals' varied pattern of responses across different situations and circumstances.

Notes

1. Nussbaum, M. C. (2001). *Upheavals of thought: The intelligence of emotions.* Cambridge: Cambridge University Press.
2. Hoffman, M. L. (2000). *Empathy and moral development: Implications for caring and justice.* Cambridge: Cambridge University Press; Turiel, E. (2006). Thought, emotions, and social interactional processes in moral development. In M. Killen & J. Smetana (Eds.), *Handbook of moral development* (pp. 7–35). Mahwah, NJ: Erlbaum.
3. Arsenio, W. F. (2010). Integrating emotion attributions, morality, and aggression: Research and theoretical foundations. In W. Arsenio & E. Lemerise (Eds.), *Emotions, aggression, and morality in children: Bridging development and psychopathology* (pp. 75–94). Washington, DC: American Psychological Association; Lemerise, E., & Maulden, J. (2010). Emotions and social information processing: Implications for understanding aggressive (and nonaggressive) children. In W. Arsenio & E. Lemerise (Eds.), *Emotions, aggression, and morality in children: Bridging development and psychopathology* (pp. 157–176). Washington, DC: American Psychological Association.
4. Arsenio. (2010); Krettenauer, T., Malti, T., & Sokol, B. W. (2008). Development of moral emotions and the happy-victimizer phenomenon: A critical review of theory and application. *European Journal of Developmental Science, 2,* 221–235; Malti, T., & Keller, M. (2010). The development of moral emotions in a cultural context. In W. Arsenio & E. Lemerise (Eds.), *Emotions, aggression, and morality in children: Bridging development and psychopathology* (pp. 177–198). Washington, DC: American Psychological Association.
5. Arsenio, W., Cooperman, S., & Lover, A. (2000). Affective predictors of preschoolers' aggression and peer acceptance: Direct and indirect effects. *Developmental Psychology, 36,* 438–448.
6. Arsenio, W., Gold, J., & Adams, E. (2006). Children's conceptions and displays of moral emotions. In M. Killen & J. Smetana (Eds.), *Handbook of moral development* (pp. 581–610). Mahwah, NJ: Erlbaum.
7. Krettenauer et al. (2008); Malti & Keller (2010); Arsenio et al. (2006).
8. Arsenio et al. (2006); Malti, T., Gasser, L., & Gutzwiller-Helfenfinger, E. (2010). Children's interpretive understanding, moral judgments, and emotion attributions: Relations to social behavior. *British Journal of Developmental Psychology, 28,* 275–292.
9. Arsenio. (2010); Arsenio, W., Gold, J., & Adams, E. (2004). Adolescents' emotion expectancies regarding aggressive and non-aggressive events: Connections with behavior problems. *Journal of Experimental Child Psychology,*

89, 338–355; Krettenauer, T., & Eichler, D. (2006). Adolescents' self-attributed moral emotions following a moral transgression: Relations with delinquency, confidence in moral judgment, and age. *British Journal of Developmental Psychology, 24*, 489–506; Krettenauer, T., Jia, F., & Mosleh, M. (2011). The role of emotion expectancies in adolescents' moral decision making. *Journal of Experimental Child Psychology, 108*, 358–370; Saelen, C., & Markovits, H. (2008). Adolescents' emotion attributions and expectations of behavior in situations involving moral conflict. *Journal of Experimental Child Psychology, 100*, 53–76.

10. Recchia, H., Wainryb, C., & Pasupathi, M. (in press). "Two for flinching": Children's and adolescents' narrative accounts of harming their friends and siblings. *Child Development*; Recchia, H., Wainryb, C., Bourne, S., & Pasupathi, M. (2012). *Children's and adolescents' accounts of helping and hurting others.* Unpublished manuscript; Wainryb, C., Brehl, B., & Matwin, S. (2005). Being hurt and hurting others: Children's narrative accounts and moral judgments of their own interpersonal conflicts. *Monographs of the Society for Research in Child Development, 70*(Serial No. 281); Wainryb, C., Komolova, M., & Brehl, B. (2012). *Being left out: Children's narrative accounts and judgments of their own experiences with peer exclusion.* Unpublished manuscript.

11. Arsenio et al. (2006).

12. Leslie, A., Mallon, R., & DiCorcia, J. (2006). Transgressors, victims, and cry-babies: Is basic moral judgment spared in autism? *Social Neuroscience, 1*, 270–283.

13. Wainryb et al. (2005); Wainryb, C. (2000). Values and truths: The making and judging of moral decisions. In M. Laupa (Ed.), *Rights and wrongs: How children evaluate the world* (pp. 33–46). San Francisco, CA: Jossey-Bass; Wainryb, C. (2011). "And so they ordered me to kill a person": Conceptualizing the impacts of child soldiering on the development of moral agency. *Human Development, 54*, 273–300.

14. Nussbaum. (2001).

15. Wainryb et al. (2005); Wainryb. (2011); Pasupathi. M., & Wainryb, C. (2010). Developing moral agency through narrative. *Human Development, 53*, 55–80; Wainryb, C., & Pasupathi, M. (2010). Political violence and disruptions in the development of moral agency. *Child Development Perspectives, 4*, 48–54.

16. Wainryb. (2011).

17. Bandura, A. (2002). Selective disengagement in the exercise of moral agency. *Journal of Moral Education, 31*, 101–119.

18. Wainryb, C., Komolova, M., & Florsheim, P. (2010). How violent youth offenders and typically developing adolescents construct moral agency in narratives about doing harm. In K. McLean & M. Pasupathi (Eds.), *Narrative and adolescent development* (pp. 185–206). New York, NY: Springer.

CECILIA WAINRYB *is a professor of psychology at the University of Utah.*

HOLLY E. RECCHIA *is an assistant professor of education at Concordia University.*

The emotion and reasoning processes involved in adolescents' experiences of moral conflict, such as intentionally harming, failing to help, or excluding others, vary across both contexts and individuals and are often associated with the individual's level of sympathy.

2

Adolescents' emotions and reasoning in contexts of moral conflict and social exclusion

Tina Malti, Sophia F. Ongley, Sebastian P. Dys, Tyler Colasante

EMOTIONS PLAY AN IMPORTANT role in adolescent moral development and morally relevant behaviors such as aggression and prosociality. How we feel about a moral conflict situation and the involved parties is likely to affect our reasoning in such situations. In turn, these feelings may influence why we adhere or fail to adhere to our own moral standards.[1] Thus, moral emotions such as guilt may serve as key motives for moral reasoning and moral action tendencies.[2]

How do adolescents feel during everyday experiences of moral conflict and social inclusion or exclusion, and how do they reason about these issues? We address these questions by integrating developmental research on emotions and reasoning in situations involving moral transgressions and social exclusion. We focus on

NEW DIRECTIONS FOR YOUTH DEVELOPMENT, NO. 136, WINTER 2012 © WILEY PERIODICALS, INC.
Published online in Wiley Online Library (wileyonlinelibrary.com) • DOI: 10.1002/yd.20036

twelve-year-old adolescents' emotions and reasoning in three contexts: intentionally harming another peer, omitting prosocial duties, and excluding another peer who is an out-group member. These contexts represent different moral and social issues and may elicit different types of emotions and reasoning.[3]

Previous developmental research has investigated how children and adolescents judge and reason about moral conflicts and social exclusion.[4] More recently, researchers have begun to integrate this social reasoning research with examinations of adolescents' emotions following everyday experiences of social exclusion.[5] However, we still know little about how adolescents coordinate emotions and reasoning about these issues, and we know even less about how their overt tendency to sympathize with others relates to their moral emotions and reasoning.

Understanding the emotions involved in experiences of morality and social exclusion is important because the development of cognition and emotion is closely interrelated in the context of moral conflict and social exclusion.[6] Likewise, the emotional ability to sympathize with others and anticipate the consequences of one's own actions for another's feelings may facilitate other-oriented, altruistic moral reasoning.

Emotions and reasoning in situations involving moral conflict and social exclusion

Emotions such as guilt are elicited when individuals feel that they have violated their own internalized moral standards. Feelings of guilt also arise when individuals develop an understanding of another person's circumstances in a conflict situation.[7] Guilt has been identified as a prototypical moral emotion. Such emotions are evoked by the individual's understanding and evaluation of the self.[8] Previous research on moral emotions has focused on the affective state that children and adolescents attribute to either hypothetical wrongdoers or to themselves in the role of wrongdoer.[9] In this paradigm, children and adolescents are typically confronted with a moral transgression, such as not keeping a promise to a friend, and are then asked how they would feel if they had been responsible for that transgression. This research has documented age-related changes in the attribution of negative (that is, moral) emotions to the self in the role of victimizer.[10] Specifically, as children get older, they increasingly attribute negative emotions to the self-as-victimizer. Research has also shown that the attribution of negative emotions is typically accompanied by moral reasons, such as empathy for the victim, fairness, and equality.[11] Although research has demonstrated that many adolescents attribute guilt or related feelings of sadness to themselves in the role of transgressor, interindividual variability remains well into midadolescence.[12] This variability suggests that in addition to developmental change, the anticipation of moral emotions is also affected by both contextual differences and interindividual differences among adolescents. Here, we investigate how both contextual and individual characteristics are related to adolescents' feelings and reasoning about moral issues. We study three morally relevant situations as contextual characteristics and sympathy as an individual characteristic.

Contextual differences in moral emotions and moral reasoning

Moral development research has revealed that children and adolescents distinguish between contexts when they make judgments about moral conflicts.[13] In this section, we investigate two well-studied moral contexts, intentional harm and the omission of prosocial duties, as well as the context of social exclusion, all in relation to emotions and reasoning.[14]

Emotions and reasoning following moral transgressions have been intensely studied in developmental research within the happy-victimizer paradigm.[15] Research in this tradition has revealed that the majority of children and adolescents evaluate others' acts of intentional harm as more severe than others' failure to perform prosocial duties. This greater severity of intentional harm, as compared to prosocial omission, has also been found when children and adolescents imagine the self as victimizer.[16]

Investigating contexts of social exclusion further elucidates children's and adolescents' emotions and reasoning about morally relevant behavior.[17] Social domain research has studied children's and adolescents' reasoning about exclusion to understand how they coordinate moral and social conventional knowledge when evaluating social events.[18]

In our own research, we have recently begun to incorporate these findings into our work on emotions. For example, we have examined how children and adolescents judge and feel about social exclusion. Samples of Swiss and non-Swiss adolescents (that is, majority and minority groups, respectively) were asked to attribute emotions to excluders or excluded individuals. Interestingly, adolescents attributed moral emotions such as guilt, as well as positively valenced, amoral emotions such as pride and happiness, to excluders. In contrast, adolescents attributed only negative emotions, such as sadness and anger, to individuals who were the victims of exclusion.[19] This finding is surprising because it suggests that adolescents are aware of the negative feelings of excluded individuals but still sometimes attribute (positive) amoral emotions to excluders. These attributions may reflect a balancing of group and moral norms. Previous research indicates that adolescents acquire an increasingly differentiated understanding of group functioning as they develop.[20] Thus, in addition to moral considerations, it is likely that group norms and group functioning are important factors in adolescents' emotions and reasoning about social exclusion.

In summary, we have a good understanding of children's and adolescents' reasoning about moral transgressions and social exclusion. Happy-victimizer research has also revealed general age-related changes from positive (immoral) to negative (moral) emotion attributions to victimizers. Yet little is known about how children and adolescents feel about contexts in which a peer is being excluded, what types of emotions adolescents anticipate in these contexts, and if these emotions are similar to or different from the ones that are anticipated when a person is being harmed or prosocial obligations are disregarded.

Adolescents' sympathy: Relations with moral emotions and moral reasoning

Sympathy entails feelings of concern for another that stem from the apprehension of the other's emotional state. Sympathy is closely related to the emotional process of empathy; however unlike empathy, sympathy does not involve feeling the same emotion as the other.[21] As such, sympathy requires rudimentary social perspective–taking skills, such as a basic understanding of the protagonist's situation and feelings, as well as how one's own actions affect these factors.[22]

Although the development of sympathy as a morally relevant process has been studied widely, it is not well known if and how adolescents with high levels of dispositional sympathy are more prone to guilt in situations entailing moral transgressions or social exclusion.

Sympathy and guilt are both considered to be morally relevant.[23] Thus, it is reasonable to assume that the ability to step into another's shoes and sympathize with his or her situation is associated with the internalization of moral norms and related feelings of guilt. However, this link has not been examined systematically. In previous research, we have investigated associations between sympathy and guilt following moral transgressions in middle childhood, but findings revealed only small to modest relations.[24]

Adolescents who generally sympathize with needy others may be more prone to anticipating negative consequences for the victim and integrating this perspective into their own affective and cognitive experiences of morally relevant conflicts. The link between sympathy and other-oriented, prosocial moral reasoning in adolescence has been empirically supported in several studies, with findings suggesting that sympathy may stimulate the use

NEW DIRECTIONS FOR YOUTH DEVELOPMENT • DOI: 10.1002/yd

of moral reasoning that is based on care and concern for others' welfare.[25]

In contrast, little is known about how sympathy relates to moral emotions and moral reasoning in the context of social exclusion. To the best of our knowledge, only one study has investigated the relation between empathy and social inclusion, in this case the inclusion of children with disabilities.[26] In this study, ten- and sixteen-year-old American and Japanese children had to respond to a situation in which a group of children wanted to go swimming and one child in a wheelchair wanted to join them. The children were asked how they would feel if the child with the disability were to join them. Results revealed that children often reported feeling empathy, acceptance of the peer with the disability, and a wish to help him or her. Here, we extend these findings and investigate how sympathy affects perceptions of and emotions associated with experiences of social exclusion.

To summarize, there is evidence that adolescents anticipate negative emotions following moral transgressions in peer relationships, and that these negative emotions are associated in meaningful ways with their reasoning about these moral issues. Conversely, evidence is lacking with respect to the types of emotions that adolescents anticipate as a result of moral transgressions, if these emotions and their justifications are similar to or different from emotions and reasoning about social exclusion, and how adolescents' general tendency to sympathize with needy others is related to their emotions and reasoning in contexts of everyday moral conflict and social exclusion.

This study

For the study described here, we were interested in investigating the following research questions:

- What kinds of emotions do adolescents attribute to themselves in the role of transgressor and excluder, and what reasons do they provide for these emotions?

- Do the emotions and reasons that are provided differ across contexts of intentional harm, omission of prosocial duties, and exclusion of an out-group peer?
- How does adolescents' overt sympathy relate to other moral emotions and moral reasoning in contexts of moral transgression and exclusion?

To address these research questions, we studied an ethnically diverse community sample of eighty-four twelve-year-old children from a major Canadian city (M age = 12.50, SD = 0.27, 42 girls). Ethnic backgrounds reported by primary caregivers were western European (32%), eastern European (13%), South and East Asian (10%), Caribbean (6%), West and Central Asian (4%), African (2%), Central and South American (1%), and other/multiple origins (28%).

Moral emotions and moral reasoning task

To measure adolescents' anticipation of moral emotions and moral reasoning, participants responded to six vignettes that were designed to elicit moral responses.[27] The vignettes represented three distinct moral contexts: failing to perform prosocial duties (for example, choosing not to share with a friend), excluding an out-group peer (for example, not letting a student new to the school join in play), and intentionally harming others (for example, pushing a classmate out of line to obtain the last candy). Following each story, participants were asked how they would feel (emotions) and why they would feel that way (reasoning).

Coding of emotions and reasoning

Anticipated emotions were coded as (1) guilt, (2) basic moral emotions (for example, sad, bad), (3) embarrassment/shame, (4) moral anger, (5) basic amoral emotions (for example, happy, good), and (6) neutral emotions (for example, feeling as usual, normal).

Justifications for emotions were assessed from an open-ended "why" question in the interview and later placed in the following categories:

- Moral reasons, which refer to norms, rules, and obligations (for example, "It is not fair to steal")
- Empathic concern for the victim (for example, "The other child will be sad")
- Sanction-oriented reasons, which refer to sanctions by an authority (for example, "The kindergarten teacher may find out and get angry")
- Hedonistic, self-serving reasons (for example, "He just likes pencils so much"
- Unelaborated and unclassifiable reasons, which reflect undifferentiated statements (for example, "It is not nice/He has the pencils")
- No reason

Interrater reliability for the coding of moral reasoning was $\kappa = .95$ (based on 15 percent of the data).

Sympathy was measured using five self-report items (for example, "When I see another child who is hurt or upset, I feel sorry for him or her").[28] Cronbach's alpha for the sympathy scale was .80.

Results

We first describe the types of emotions that young adolescents attributed to themselves in the role of victimizer/excluder for the three contexts. Figure 2.1 shows that adolescents anticipate a wide range of emotions across contexts, including complex moral emotions such as guilt, anger, embarrassment and shame, and basic moral and amoral emotions such as sad or bad, happy or good, and neutral emotion. The anticipation of several emotions varied across contexts, including feeling guilty, $F (2, 652) = 15.82, p < .001$, sad/bad, $F (2, 652) = 8.43, p < .001$, happy/good, $F (2, 652) = 3.39, p < .05$, and neutral, $F (2, 652) = 7.44, p < .001$. Guilt was anticipated more frequently after imagining intentional harm than after social exclusion or prosocial omission ($ps < .001$), whereas more basic moral emotions (sad or bad) were anticipated more often in contexts of social exclusion and prosocial omission

Figure 2.1. Adolescents' emotions following intentional harm, omission of prosocial duties, and social exclusion

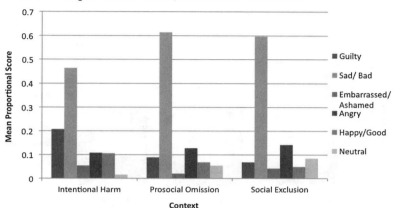

($p < .01, p < .001$, respectively). Positive emotions (happy or good) were anticipated more frequently in contexts of causing intentional harm than in contexts of social exclusion ($p < .05$), and neutral feelings were anticipated more frequently after participants imagined excluding an out-group peer than after causing intentional harm ($p < .001$).

Adolescents' reasons for their emotion attributions provided additional information on the motives underlying their affective states. Findings revealed that the majority of adolescents were concerned about moral issues such as fairness or equality (Figure 2.2). In the words of one adolescent, "I wasn't treating everyone equally. Since she was new, she probably didn't have anyone to hang out with, and I made it worse." Many adolescents also provided reasons based on empathy toward others—for example, "When somebody don't want to play and another person comes and you say no, it hurts." Adolescents also provided hedonistic and sanction-based reasons for their anticipated emotions.

There were significant differences in the use of different types of reasoning depending on the type of transgression. Specifically, moral reasons were more frequent in contexts of intentional harm than in contexts of prosocial omission or exclusion ($ps < .001$),

Figure 2.2. Adolescents' reasons following intentional harm, omission of prosocial duties, and social exclusion

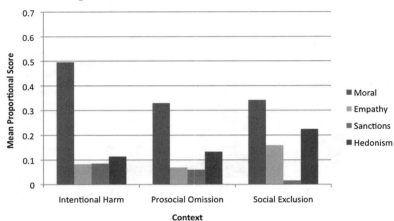

whereas hedonistic reasons were more frequent after contexts of social exclusion ($p < .001$, $p < .05$) than after contexts of intentional harm and prosocial omission, respectively. Interestingly, social exclusion contexts elicited empathy-based reasoning more frequently than either intentional harm or prosocial omission contexts ($p < .05$, $p < .01$, respectively), while reasoning based on sanctions or rules was more common in contexts of intentional harm than in contexts of social exclusion, $p < .01$.

Adolescents' sympathy was associated with emotions in situations of moral conflict and social exclusion, and with the reasons they provided for their affective state. To assess the role of sympathy in adolescents' emotion attributions, we examined whether each emotion attribution was anticipated differentially for adolescents who were low (at least 1 *SD* below the mean), average (within 1 *SD* of the mean), or high in sympathy (at least 1 *SD* above the mean). There were significant differences across the three levels of sympathy in the anticipation of guilt ($F (2, 622) = 4.23$, $p < .05$), anger, ($F (2, 622) = 3.11$, $p < .05$), and positive emotions, such as feeling happy or good, ($F (2, 622) = 3.68$, $p < .05$). Moral anger on behalf of the victims was anticipated more frequently by adolescents with high levels of sympathy, as was the moral emotion of guilt. By contrast, amoral positive emotions (happy, good) were associated with low levels of sympathy. In addition, moral reasoning occurred more often among adolescents with higher sympathy $(F(2, 584) = 3.00, p = .05)$, while hedonistic reasoning occurred more often among adolescents with lower sympathy $(F(2, 584) = 8.09, p < .001)$.

Conclusion

We studied the types of emotions that adolescents anticipate when violating moral rules or excluding a peer, as well as the justifications they provide for these emotions. We also investigated the role of sympathy in adolescents' anticipation of and reasoning about morally relevant emotions.

Our findings showed that young adolescents anticipate a wide range of negatively valenced emotions in contexts of moral transgressions and social exclusion and, to a lesser extent, positively valenced and neutral (amoral) emotions. Adolescents' negative emotions were primarily accompanied by moral justifications, including concerns about fairness and equality. Interestingly, most adolescents also viewed excluding others as causing negative emotions in the self, and these emotions were justified by moral and empathic concerns. In addition, adolescents' anticipation of emotions, and the reasons they use to justify these emotions, differed across contexts of moral transgression and social exclusion. Whereas contexts of intentional harm elicited complex moral emotions (guilt) and amoral positive emotions (feeling happy or good), contexts of prosocial omission and social exclusion more frequently elicited basic moral emotions (feeling sad). In combination with the greater use of moral reasoning in contexts of intentional harm, these findings suggest that adolescents view acts of intentional harm as more serious and morally relevant than the failure to help, share, or include others. Interestingly, the context of social exclusion elicited the highest levels of both empathy-based and hedonistic reasoning, suggesting that concerns over personal gains and group functioning compete with concerns of fairness and empathy in decisions to exclude or include peers.

We found evidence suggesting that overt sympathy plays an important role in adolescents' emotion attributions and reasoning in moral conflict situations. High levels of sympathy were associated with emotions and justifications that emphasized the wrongfulness of hypothetical transgressions. For example, adolescents with high levels of sympathy anticipated guilt and moral anger over transgressions more often than those who were low in sympathy. Inversely, adolescents who were low in sympathy were more likely than those with high levels of sympathy to experience positive, amoral emotions after imagining moral transgressions and social exclusion. Consistent with associations between sympathy and anticipated emotion, findings regarding sympathy and reasoning showed that highly sympathetic adolescents were more likely to use moral reasons to justify their emotions, whereas those who were low in sympathy were more likely to justify their emotion attributions with hedonistic reasoning focused on personal gains. Thus, these findings support the view that emotions and cognitions about moral issues may be integrated into one's identity by early adolescence, which leads to more consistency between different moral emotions and moral reasoning.[29]

Further research on early, mid-, and late adolescence is warranted to address developmental similarities and differences in emotions and reasoning about everyday experiences of moral conflict and social exclusion. Emotions are important for adolescents' reasoning and morally relevant behavior. Studying these affective experiences can help us understand why adolescents think and act the way they do in critical, everyday situations of moral and social conflict.

Notes

1. Tangney, J. P., Stuewig, J., & Mashek, D. J. (2007). Moral emotions and moral behavior. *Annual Review of Psychology*, *58*, 345–372.

2. Arsenio, W., Gold, J., & Adams, E. (2006). Children's conceptions and displays of moral emotions. In M. Killen & J. Smetana (Eds.), *Handbook of moral development* (1st ed., pp. 581–610). Mahwah, NJ: Erlbaum.

3. Smetana, J. G. (2006). Social-cognitive domain theory: Consistencies and variations in children's moral and social judgments. In M. Killen & J. G. Smetana (Eds.), *Handbook of moral development* (1st ed., pp. 119–153). Mahwah, NJ: Erlbaum.

4. Keller, M. (2004). Self in relationship. In D. K. Lapsley & D. Narvaez (Eds.), *Morality, self, and identity* (pp. 269–300). Mahwah, NJ: Erlbaum; Killen, M., Lee-Kim, J., McGlothlin, H., & Stangor, C. (2002). How children and adolescents evaluate gender and racial exclusion. *Monographs for the Society for Research in Child Development* (Serial No. 271, Vol. 67, No. 4). Oxford, England: Blackwell.

5. Malti, T., & Ongley, S. (in press). The development of moral emotions and moral reasoning. In M. Killen & J. Smetana (Eds.), *Handbook of moral development* (2nd ed.). New York, NY: Taylor & Francis.

6. Malti, T., & Latzko, B. (2012). Moral emotions. In V. Ramachandran (Ed.), *Encyclopedia of human behavior* (2nd ed., pp. 644–649). Maryland Heights, MO: Elsevier.

7. Malti, T., & Keller, M. (2010). Development of moral emotions in cultural context. In W. Arsenio & E. Lemerise (Eds.), *Emotions, aggression, and morality in children: Bridging development and psychopathology* (pp. 177–198). Washington, DC: American Psychological Association.

8. Eisenberg, N. (2000). Emotion, regulation, and moral development. *Annual Review of Psychology, 51*, 665–697; Tangney et al. (2007).

9. Arsenio et al. (2006); Krettenauer, T., & Eichler, D. (2006). Adolescents' self-attributed emotions following a moral transgression: Relations with delinquency, confidence in moral judgment, and age. *British Journal of Developmental Psychology, 24*, 489–506.

10. Keller, M., Lourenço, S., Malti, T., & Saalbach, H. (2003). The multifaceted phenomenon of "happy victimizers": A cross-cultural comparison of moral emotions. *British Journal of Developmental Psychology, 21*, 1–18.

11. Gasser, L., & Keller, M. (2009). Are the competent the morally good? Perspective taking and moral motivation of children involved in bullying. *Social Development, 18*, 798–816.

12. Krettenauer, T., & Eichler, D. (2006). Adolescents' self-attributed emotions following a moral transgression: Relations with delinquency, confidence in moral judgment, and age. *British Journal of Developmental Psychology, 24*, 489–506.

13. Smetana. (2006).

14. Malti, T., Gummerum, M., Keller, M., & Buchmann, M. (2009). Children's moral motivation, sympathy, and prosocial behavior. *Child Development, 80*, 442–460; Killen et al. (2002).

15. For a review, see Arsenio et al. (2006).

16. Malti et al. (2009).

17. Hitti, A., Lynn Mulvey, K., & Killen, M. (2011). Social exclusion and culture: The role of group norms, group identity and fairness. *Anales de Psicologia, 27*(3), 587–599.

18. Killen et al. (2002).

19. Malti, T., Killen, M., & Gasser, L. (2012). Social judgments and emotion attributions about exclusion in Switzerland. *Child Development, 83*, 697–711.

20. Abrams, D., Rutland, A., Pelletier, J., & Ferrell, J. M. (2009). Children's group nous: Understanding and applying peer exclusion within and between groups. *Child Development, 80*, 224–243.

21. Eisenberg. (2000).

22. Malti & Ongley. (in press).

23. Hoffman, M. L. (2000). *Empathy and moral development: Implications for caring and justice*. Cambridge: Cambridge University Press.

24. Malti et al. (2009).

25. Carlo, G., Mestre, M. V., Samper, P., Tur, A., & Armenta, B. E. (2010). The longitudinal relations among dimensions of parenting styles, sympathy, prosocial moral reasoning, and prosocial behaviors. *International Journal of Behavioral Development, 35*(2), 116–124.

26. Crystal, D. S., Watanabe, H., & Chen, R. (1999). Children's reactions to physical disability: A cross-national and developmental study. *International Journal of Behavioral Development, 23*, 99–111.

27. Malti, T. (2011). *The moral emotion attribution instrument*. Unpublished instrument, University of Toronto.

28. Zhou, Q., Valiente, C., & Eisenberg, N. (2003). Empathy and its measurement. In S. J. Lopez & C. R. Snyder (Eds.), *Positive psychological assessment: A handbook of models and measures* (pp. 269–284). Washington, DC: American Psychological Association.

29. Malti & Latzko. (2012).

TINA MALTI *is an assistant professor of developmental and clinical child psychology at the University of Toronto. She also holds an affiliate scientist position at the Jacobs Center for Productive Youth Development in Switzerland.*

SOPHIA F. ONGLEY *is a graduate student in the developmental program at the Graduate School of Psychology, University of Toronto.*

SEBASTIAN P. DYS *is a graduate student in the developmental program at the Graduate School of Psychology, University of Toronto.*

TYLER COLASANTE *is a graduate student in the developmental program at the Graduate School of Psychology, University of Toronto.*

Adolescents use emotional evaluations and moral judgments in the context of intergroup social exclusion.

3

Moral judgments and emotions: Adolescents' evaluations in intergroup social exclusion contexts

Shelby Cooley, Laura Elenbaas, Melanie Killen

REASONING AND EMOTION in humans are often conceptualized as opposite ends of a spectrum, with emotions perceived as instinctual, reflexive, or automatic and reasoning perceived as learned, deliberate, or intentional. However, in contrast to this dichotomous perspective, considerable research supports the view that emotions and reasoning are reciprocal and complementary, and both play important roles as sources of information and the basis for judgments and action in morally relevant social contexts.[1] We propose that emotions and judgments are linked in children's and adolescents' social interpretations of events in daily life. Experiencing an emotion often involves a cognitive appraisal of a situation, and subsequent appraisals are reciprocally influenced by emotional experiences. Both emotions and judgments are important for understanding the development of morality in adolescence, particularly in complex social contexts in which group membership and allegiance are in contrast to morally relevant decisions, like the exclusion of an individual from a social group.[2]

NEW DIRECTIONS FOR YOUTH DEVELOPMENT, NO. 136, WINTER 2012 © WILEY PERIODICALS, INC.
Published online in Wiley Online Library (wileyonlinelibrary.com) • DOI: 10.1002/yd.20037

Adolescence is often characterized as a time of emotional turbulence, hormonal changes, and teen rebellion against parents. However, this perspective fails to account for the reflection and development of ideologies that occur during this period.[3] Adolescence is also a time when youth establish a strong sense of group affiliation that has significant implications for their developing principles of fairness, justice, and equality.[4] However, not enough research has examined the reciprocal nature of moral judgments and emotions during adolescence, and even less work has examined these variables in a social exclusion context.[5]

Throughout development, emotions are central to making morally relevant evaluations and attributions in social contexts.[6] Emotions provide important information when reading social cues, recalling experiences, and deciding how to respond in social interactions.[7] As peer contexts become increasingly meaningful in adolescence, youth begin to weigh moral and emotional judgments in complex ways as issues of group identity and group loyalty are brought to bear on morally salient decisions.[8]

In this article, we first review current research on the role of emotions in moral judgments during adolescence, highlighting work that sheds new light on the complex context of intergroup social exclusion. We then explore new directions for future research on intergroup social exclusion in adolescence that draw on the increasing salience of group membership in youth and the consequences of individual resistance to group norms. We introduce a research agenda focused on understanding young people's moral judgments and emotions in these complex social contexts.

Developmental origins of moral judgments and emotions

Adolescents' evaluations of others' emotional states and anticipations of the effects of social interactions or moral violations are key to moral development as these emotional judgments pertain to issues of fairness, justice, harm, and rights. To understand the relationship between emotions and judgments in adolescence, it is valuable to understand the precursors or building blocks, that is, the foundations of morality prior to adolescence.

From a young age, sympathy and empathy emerge as components of early morality that involve both emotions and judgments.[9] From as young as fourteen months, infants and young children have been shown to demonstrate empathy and sympathy and to cooperate with peers and adults who share a common goal.[10] For example, toddlers' emotional responses (facial, vocal, and gestural expressions of concern) toward an individual feigning pain increase with age, suggesting that experiences of empathic arousal (especially within the context of adult guidance) promote moral development.[11]

Research suggests that young children understand moral behavior through experience with negative emotions such as guilt, fear, and anxiety.[12] However, research also indicates that a wider range of emotions (not only negative feelings) is important for children's social-emotional and moral growth.[13] Thus, there is clear evidence for the coexistence of both positive (favorability, pride, happiness) and negative emotions in children's lives and for the relevance of both in the acquisition of morality. In the next section, we explore how emotions and judgments are interwoven in adolescents' evaluations of complex social exchanges, particularly exchanges that involve exclusion and intergroup attitudes.

Social exclusion: Types and consequences

Peer rejection and social exclusion, ubiquitous throughout childhood and adolescence, present a critical context to examine social, moral, and emotional development. One type of research on peer rejection in childhood and adolescence focuses on interpersonal social exclusion. In this context, individual differences such as temperament and social-emotional traits contribute to maladaptive peer relationships and the rejection of one individual by another.[14]

In instances of interpersonal social exclusion, the rejected individual is described as shy, fearful, or lacking in social skills, and the individual who initiates the rejection is one who habitually engages in bullying and is often found to be extremely aggressive. As a consequence of exclusion, rejected children and adolescents suffer from depression, loneliness, social withdrawal, and poor academic achievement.[15]

Witnessing the exclusion of an individual from a group can elicit emotional responses of empathy or sympathy in adolescence, but understanding the context and criteria for exclusion is essential for determining the moral relevance of the act.[16] In some cases, an act of rejection that is interpreted as interpersonal by one person could be interpreted as intergroup by another, and would be a wrong appraisal. For example, rejecting a peer from a swim team may involve interpersonal rejection; however, if the team is ethnic majority and the excluded member is ethnic minority, then the context creates a different factor, which is also intergroup (not just interpersonal). As an illustration, an adolescent might feel empathy for a poor swimmer who is excluded from a high school varsity swim team but also view this exclusion as legitimate. In contrast, the same adolescent might feel empathy for a black student who is excluded from the swim team because of a belief that black people cannot swim and also view this type of exclusion as discriminatory and thus morally wrong. Research has provided evidence for this distinction in terms of individuals' affective responses to exclusion and subsequent emotional judgments of the excluding group. For example, Nesdale et al. examined social exclusion on the basis of school membership (intergroup exclusion) and perceived drawing talent (interpersonal exclusion) with a sample of six- and eight-year-old Australian children.[17] Participants who were rejected for an intergroup reason (school membership) reported greater dislike of the rejecting group than children who were rejected for an interpersonal (drawing talent) reason. Although both types of social exclusion caused distress for participants, this study highlights the importance of affective experiences and social-cognitive judgments in determining the moral relevance of exclusion in intergroup contexts.

In contrast to research on interpersonal rejection, research on intergroup exclusion addresses the macro, societal-level structures of prejudice, bias, power, and status that emerge early in childhood and result in group-based rejection.[18] The emotional consequences of exclusion on the basis of group membership are severe, as individuals under these circumstances experience discrimination and rejection as a result of stereotypes, prejudice, and bias that can lead to anxiety, depression, social withdrawal, and academic risk factors.[19] Research on adolescents in the United States has indicated that experiences of discrimination based on racial/ethnic group membership differ across groups, with participants of Latin American and Asian backgrounds reporting more experiences of discrimination from adults and peers than their European American peers. Frequency of discrimination has been found to predict lower grade point average, lower self-esteem, and more depressive symptoms, distress, and physical complaints.[20] Furthermore, the existence and status of various types of groups in an individual's environment can also play a role in understanding the impact of discrimination on adolescent well-being. For example, Graham et al. found that for a sample of Latino and African American adolescents, self-blame (for one's own experience of social exclusion) partially explained the relationship between victimization and maladjustment when participants were members of the racial/ethnic majority at their school but not when participants were members of the racial/ethnic minority.[21]

The caustic consequences of discrimination underscore the importance of understanding adolescents' emotions, evaluations, and social-cognitive reasoning about discrimination in their lives. Youths' understanding and perceptions of discrimination are shaped by age-related changes in their cognitive skills as they shift from a focus on the relation between individuals' intergroup biases and their discriminatory behavior to acknowledgment of the role of society and the unjust systems of oppression that perpetuate discrimination.[22]

Intergroup social exclusion in adolescence: A theoretical model

When young people make decisions about social exclusion or evaluate the exclusion decisions of others, they integrate their affective experiences, social-cognitive attributions of the emotions and intentions of others, and moral reasoning capabilities. Although adolescence is often characterized as a period of group conformity, research indicates that with age, youth become increasingly aware of the moral and emotional consequences of social exclusion on the basis of group membership, strengthening their evaluation of such exclusion as wrong.[23] In this section, we highlight recent research on intergroup social exclusion in adolescence that illustrates how emotions and moral judgments intertwine in this context.

Killen and her colleagues have investigated intergroup social exclusion by drawing on social domain theory as well as social identity theory and identifying a new perspective, which they refer to as a social reasoning developmental model.[24] Traditionally, social domain theory identified three domains as central to social evaluations of everyday events:

- The moral domain, which refers to issues of justice, others' welfare, and rights, in which interindividual treatment results in a victim deprived of rights or resources
- The societal domain, which refers to conventions, traditions, and customs determined by social consensus and designed to make groups work well (these do not have moral consequences)
- The psychological domain, which refers to personal choice (decisions that are not regulated but viewed as a matter of individual preferences)[25]

Social identity theory provided a model for evaluating the degree to which an adolescent's group identity bears on his or her evaluations of intergroup social exclusion. In-group identity emerges early in development and is related to out-group derogation in that motivation to enhance the in-group results in dislike of the out-group under conditions of threat. Developmental social identity research has shown that the degree to which a child or adolescent identifies with a group is related to his or her emerging prejudice and bias.[26]

Studies incorporating both social identity theory and social domain theory led to the social reasoning model, which expanded the content of the domain categories for the area of intergroup exclusion to include the wrongfulness of discrimination (*moral*), group functioning and group identity (*societal*), and intentionality (*psychological*) that is central to the social evaluations of multifaceted and complex events. Research has demonstrated that social exclusion is variably viewed as wrong (unfair), legitimate (for group functioning), or a personal choice. The contextual features that are related to different forms of reasoning include the complexity or ambiguity of a situation, along with other information, such as knowledge and prior experience, as well as group goals.[27] Research questions have pertained to the degree to which identification with a group is related to social reasoning about intergroup exclusion.[28] Furthermore, current research has also applied this model to group membership contexts beyond those of race and ethnicity and has expanded the study of intergroup social exclusion to the context of school groups, nationality, religion, gender, and sexual orientation.

Across samples of European American, African American, Asian American, Latin American, and multiracial adolescents, ratings of the wrongfulness of race-based social exclusion, for example, have been found to increase with age; participants judged such exclusion to be wrong on the moral grounds of unfair treatment. The role of group membership status, however, is significant in these contexts. When examining racial/ethnic minority and majority children's evaluations of race-based exclusion, racial/ethnic minority children were found to evaluate exclusion as more wrong than did racial/ethnic majority children.[29] A similar age-related pattern emerges with regard to adolescents' decisions regarding the acceptability of excluding an individual from an activity on the basis of sexual orientation; such exclusion is viewed as increasingly wrong with age on the moral grounds of human equality and fairness.[30]

When examining multidimensional frameworks of group membership, adolescents demonstrate an increasing capacity to weigh the impact of exclusion based on different types of group membership. For example, Danish majority adolescents have been found to differentiate exclusion on the basis of gender and ethnicity, deeming exclusion based on gender to be more acceptable (for conventional reasons) than exclusion based on ethnicity (which was condemned for moral reasons).[31] Similarly, ethnic majority Dutch and minority Turkish adolescents have been found to judge the exclusion of someone who shared their gender and ethnicity to be worse than the exclusion of someone with whom they shared only one or no common in-group. These adolescents also evaluated excluders who shared their gender and ethnicity less harshly than excluders with whom they shared only one or no common in-group.[32] These results begin to elaborate the complexities of group dynamics in adolescence and the ways in which group membership influences adolescents' emotional and cognitive appraisals of intergroup social exclusion situations. Though the context is morally salient, decisions in such social situations are multifaceted.

Significant strides have been made toward understanding the reciprocal nature of reasoning and emotion in the morally salient context of intergroup social exclusion. However, few studies have directly assessed both judgments and emotions in the context of group-based social exclusion. One exception is a recent study by Malti, Killen, and Gasser in which both social cognition related to participants' evaluations of exclusion and emotional attributions to the individuals involved were directly examined in regard to exclusion on both an interpersonal and intergroup basis.[33] In this study, adolescents of native Swiss and other non-Swiss nationalities evaluated the exclusion of an individual on the basis of gender, nationality (Serbian or Swiss), or personality. Overall, exclusion based on nationality (a type of group membership) was judged to be less acceptable than exclusion based on personality (an individual characteristic), and this distinction was particularly strong for non-Swiss participants. Participants overall thought that the individual who excluded another would feel pride, happiness, guilt, shame, and empathy, and the excluded individual would feel sadness and anger, but non-Swiss participants were noted to attribute more positive emotions to the excluding character than did Swiss participants. This study illustrated the interplay of emotions and cognitive judgments as young people consider the sensitive issue of exclusion on the basis of group membership.

The questions of group membership, multiple group membership, and group status make decisions regarding exclusion of an individual based on group affiliation complex. In addition to these variables, adolescents must also consider the current affective state of relations between groups. Intergroup relations are not always negative, and in fact the norms that a group has about attitudes toward and treatment of individuals from other groups have been found to be influential in individuals' perceptions of out-groups. Research on intergroup contact has established that intergroup interactions under conditions in which both groups share common goals and cooperate, and in which both groups have equal status and institutional/authority support, decrease biases and promote harmonious social relationships.[34]

These norms and affective states can be manipulated experimentally in order to understand their impact on several levels across development. For example, Anglo Australian children in an intergroup drawing competition relate differently to their competing team with age. Seven year olds reported dislike for the competing team in all cases except when their team held a norm of inclusion (liked people who were different) and the competing team was nonthreatening; in this case, seven year olds liked the competing team. In contrast, nine year olds were neutral toward the competing team in all cases except when their team held a norm of exclusion (did not like people who are different) and the competing team threatened the participant's team (said they were "out to get" them); in this case nine year olds disliked the competing team.[35] In sum, children as young as seven years of age are able to coordinate information as nuanced as the emotional relations between groups, the moral norms that groups hold, and overarching social category memberships. These components of intergroup relations contribute to young people's perceptions and emotional evaluations of intergroup social exclusion.

―――――――

Intergroup social exclusion: Adolescents' evaluations of group nonconformists

Research on social exclusion in adolescence that takes into account both moral reasoning and emotional attributions contributes to an especially rich understanding of the interplay of reasoning and emotion and bridges the gap between these often dissociated constructs in research on intergroup relations. Just as group membership cannot be reduced to an individual's identification with a single overarching societal grouping like race/ethnicity, nationality, gender, or sexual orientation, the decision about whether to exclude an individual from a group hinges on all of these factors, as well as the in-group and out-group attitudes or norms held by the groups in question.[36] Yet not all members of groups conform to group norms. When an individual's group loyalty is called into question (e.g., a member going against his or her group's norm), adolescents' capacity to recognize and evaluate that individual and his or her actions in the context of the group gives us greater insight into moral development in youth. Research in this domain investigates individuals' perceptions of group nonconformists, their actions, and what their group should do as a result. How do adolescents feel about individuals who dissent from (or do not conform to) a group's customs or beliefs? How do these feelings vary based on the moral relevance of the nonconformist's actions (Was he or she standing up against a negative group norm)? When do adolescents make the decision to exclude someone who is going against the norms of their group? How do these decisions and the reasons for them vary based on the moral relevance of the nonconformist's actions (Was he or she undercutting a positive group norm)?

NEW DIRECTIONS FOR YOUTH DEVELOPMENT • DOI: 10.1002/yd

It has been argued that social change comes about by resisting group norms that violate moral principles of fairness, justice, and rights.[37] Throughout adolescence, youth are confronted with groups in which norms and behavior are in contrast to the moral values of justice, fairness, and human rights. In these instances, when a group promotes inequality or injustice, deviance from such a group *is* morally warranted. Recent work by Killen et al. established a paradigm for investigating the interplay among the social norms of groups, exclusion decisions, and group identity.[38] Building from this paradigm, findings from Hitti et al. examined when youth judged the act of excluding a deviant member of a group as wrong and found that children and adolescents' own affective evaluations of the nonconformist predicted variance in their judgments of exclusion.[39]

To illustrate our points about emotions and moral judgments in an intergroup context, findings from Hitti et al. regarding the influence of group norms on adolescents' emotional evaluations of nonconformists and evaluations of exclusion will be briefly reviewed.[40] In this study, U.S. participants aged nine to ten years and thirteen to fourteen years were introduced to age- and gender-matched groups that held norms about moral issues pertaining to the distribution of important resources (money) and a nonconformist who went against the group norm by advocating the opposite perspective. Participants were asked how much they liked each nonconformist (individual favorability: "How much do you like or not like the nonconformist?"). How much participants like the target is an emotion-based evaluation in contrast to a moral judgment which refers to whether the act of exclusion is all right or not all right. As an example, one may like someone who does something that is viewed as wrong from a moral viewpoint; alternatively, one may dislike someone who does something that is viewed as right from a moral viewpoint. Thus, in addition to favorability assessments, participants were asked whether the act of exclusion was all right or not all right (acceptability of exclusion: "How okay or not okay is it for the group to exclude the nonconformist?").

In examining the relationship between how much participants liked a nonconformist and whether they thought it was acceptable to exclude that person, responses were linked such that participants who reported not liking the nonconformist also found it more acceptable for the group to exclude him or her (Figure 3.1). While participants found it more acceptable for the group to exclude a nonconformist if they themselves did not like this member, the degree of their acceptability varied by the type of nonconformist (or type of belief endorsed by the nonconformist). Participants who did not like the nonconformist who advocated for an unequal distribution, when the group held an equal norm, rated the group's decision to exclude that person significantly different from "neutral," suggesting that in this case, youth affirmed the group's decision to exclude. Thus, this unequal nonconformist, though he or she would advantage the group by suggesting that the person received more money than another group, went against the group's equal norm. Participants who did not like this member also felt that the group's decision to exclude the unequal nonconformist was warranted. Evaluations were different, however, for the

Figure 3.1. Emotional evaluations of group nonconformists and judgments about the act of exclusion

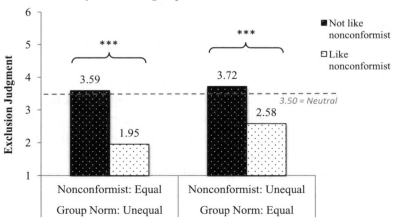

nonconformist who espoused equality. Youth who did not like the equal nonconformist evaluated the group's decision to exclude this member to be neutral: they did not accept or reject the group's decision to exclude. Perhaps this case presented a moral tension; here the nonconformist advocated for equal distribution of money (putting him or her in the moral right), yet doing so went against a group norm.

These results indicate a tension between the emotional evaluations of those who resist a group's norm and their judgments about the social exclusion of such individuals. In contrast to other work on intergroup social exclusion (referenced in the preceding sections), the young people in this study did not always exhibit increasing disapproval of social exclusion with age. In fact, no age findings were confirmed in these analyses. Both children and adolescents' feelings toward the nonconformist were not always in harmony with their opinions regarding the exclusion of that individual from the group, as evidenced by their evaluations of excluding an equal nonconforming group member.

Overall, these results suggest youth to be proficient at dually engaging norms about the expectations of their social group with the overarching moral norms of society. They recognized the tension between group norms and societal expectations. Children's and adolescents' moral evaluations of a nonconformist and their judgments regarding the acceptability of exclusion of this individual reveal their joint concern for group identity and morality.

Conclusion

Issues of inclusion and exclusion are central to social life. Adolescents frequently experience complex social situations involving peer pressure and group membership that reflect conflicting messages, goals, and norms. In cases in which members of their own group espouse norms that go against moral values like fairness, justice, and rights, the decision of what to do, whether exclusion is justified, and whether this type of deviance changes one's favorability toward one's peer or the group is difficult.[41] Understanding the emotion attributions as well as the social evaluations of these types of encounters provide new insights regarding the integration of emotional evaluations and moral judgments in the context of social exclusion. Ultimately a central challenge for development is to determine when morality takes priority over group loyalty and what to do in cases in which a conflict exists. Studying these social cognitive judgments and processes in adolescence will help to create programs to ameliorate prejudicial attitudes that if left unchecked in adolescence, create tensions and problems in the adult world of the workforce. Creating a just and fair society requires attending to the social developmental origins of fairness and facilitating positive social development.

Notes

1. Arsenio, W. F., & Lover, A. (1995). Children's conceptions of sociomoral affect: Happy victimizers, mixed emotions, and other expectancies. In M. Killen & D. Hart (Eds.), *Morality in everyday life* (pp. 87–128). Cambridge: Cambridge University Press; Malti, T., Killen, M., & Gasser, L. (2012). Social judgments and emotion attributions about exclusion in Switzerland. *Child Development, 83*, 697–771.

2. Turiel, E., & Killen, M. (2010). Taking emotions seriously: The role of emotions in moral development. In W. Arsenio & E. Lemerise (Eds.), *Emotions in aggression and moral development* (pp. 33–52). Washington, DC: APA.

3. Smetana, J. G. (2011). *Adolescents, families, and social development: How teens construct their worlds.* Hoboken, NJ: Wiley/Blackwell.

4. Killen, M., & Rutland, A. (2011). *Children and social exclusion: Morality, prejudice, and group identity.* Hoboken, NJ: Wiley/Blackwell.

5. Eisenberg, N., Spinard, T. L., & Sadovsky, A. (2006). Empathy-related responding in children. In M. Killen & J. G. Smetana (Eds.), *Handbook of moral development* (pp. 517–549). Mahwah, NJ: Erlbaum.

6. Shaw, L. A., & Wainryb, C. (2006). When victims don't cry: Children's understandings of victimization, compliance, and subversion. *Child Development, 77*, 1050–1062.

7. Arsenio, W. F., & Lemerise, E. A. (2004). Aggression and moral development: Integrating social information processing and moral domain models. *Child Development, 75*, 987–1002.

8. Killen, M., Hitti, A., & Mulvey, K. L. (in press). Social development and intergroup relations. In J. Simpson & J. Dovidio (Eds.), *APA handbook of personality and social psychology, Vol. 2. Interpersonal relations and group processes.* Washington, DC: APA Press.

9. Eisenberg et al. (2006).

10. Rhodes, M., & Brickman, D. (2011). The influence of competition on children's social categories. *Journal of Cognition and Development*, *12*(2), 194–221. doi:10.1080/15248372.2010.535230; Warneken, F., & Tomasello, M. (2006). Altruistic helping in human infants and young chimpanzees. *Science*, *311*(5765), 1301–1303. doi:10.1126/science.1121448

11. Rhodes & Brickman. (2011); Thompson, R. A., Meyer, S., & McGinley, M. (2006). Understanding values in relationships: The development of conscience. In M. Killen & J. G. Smetana (Eds.), *Handbook of moral development* (pp. 267–297). Mahwah, NJ: Erlbaum.

12. Hastings, P. D., Zahn-Waxler, C., & McShane, K. (2006). We are, by nature, moral creatures: Biological bases of concern for others. In M. Killen & J. G. Smetana (Eds.), *Handbook of moral development*. Mahwah, NJ: Erlbaum.

13. Dunn, J. (2006). Moral development in early childhood and social interaction in the family. In M. Killen & J. G. Smetana (Eds.), *Handbook of moral development* (pp. 331–350). Mahwah, NJ: Erlbaum; Thompson et al. (2006).

14. Bierman, K. L. (2004). *Peer rejection: Developmental processes and intervention strategies*. New York, NY: Guilford Press; Rubin, K., Bukowski, W., & Parker, J. (2006). Peers, relationships, and interactions. In W. Damon & R. Lerner (Eds.), *Handbook of child psychology* (pp. 571–645). Hoboken, NJ: Wiley.

15. Bierman. (2004).

16. Malti et al. (2012).

17. Nesdale, D., Maass, A., Kiesner, J., Durkin, K., Griffiths, J., & Ekberg, A. (2007). Effects of peer group rejection, group membership, and group norms, on children's outgroup prejudice. *International Journal of Behavioral Development*, *31*(5), 526–535. doi:10.1177/0165025407081479

18. Kinzler, K. D., & DeJesus, J. (in press). Children's sociolinguistic evaluations of nice foreigners and mean Americans. *Developmental Psychology*.

19. Huynh, V. W., & Fuligni, A. J. (2010). Discrimination hurts: The academic, psychological, and physical well-being of adolescents. *Journal of Research on Adolescence*, *20*(4), 916–941. doi:10.1111/j.1532-7795.2010.00670.x

20. Huynh & Fuligni. (2010).

21. Graham, S., Bellmore, A., Nishina, A., & Juvonen, J. (2009). "It must be me": Ethnic diversity and attributions for peer victimization in middle school. *Journal of Youth and Adolescence*, *38*(4), 487–499. doi:10.1007/s10964-008-9386-4

22. Brown, C. S., & Bigler, R. (2005). Children's perceptions of discrimination: A developmental model. *Child Development*, *76*, 533–553.

23. Smetana. (2011); Horn, S. (2003). Adolescents' reasoning about exclusion from social groups. *Developmental Psychology*, *39*, 71–84; Horn, S. S., Szalacha, L. A., & Drill, K. (2008). Schooling, sexuality, and rights: An investigation of heterosexual students' social cognition regarding sexual orientation and the rights of gay and lesbian peers in school. *Journal of Social Issues*, *64*(4), 791–813. doi:10.1111/j.1540-4560.2008.00589.x; Killen, M., Henning, A., Kelly, M. C., Crystal, D., & Ruck, M. (2007). Evaluations of

interracial peer encounters by majority and minority US children and adolescents. *International Journal of Behavioral Development*, *31*, 491–500. doi:10.1177/0165025407081478

24. Killen, M., & Rutland, A. (2011); Rutland, A., Killen, M., & Abrams, D. (2010). A new social-cognitive developmental perspective on prejudice: The interplay between morality and group identity. *Perspectives on Psychological Science*, *5*(3), 279–291. doi:10.1177/1745691610369468; Tajfel, H., & Turner, J. C. (1979). An integrative theory of intergroup conflict. In W. G. Austin & S. Worchel (Eds.), *The social psychology of intergroup relations* (pp. 33–47). Monterey, CA: Brooks-Cole; Turiel, E. (1983). *The development of social knowledge: Morality and convention*. Cambridge: Cambridge University Press; Turiel, E. (2002). *The culture of morality: Social development, context, and conflict*. Cambridge: Cambridge University Press.

25. Turiel. (1983).

26. Nesdale, D. (2008). Social identity development and children's ethnic attitudes in Australia. In S. Quintana & C. McKown (Eds.), *Handbook of race, racism and the developing child* (pp. 313–338). Hoboken, NJ: Wiley; Rutland et al. (2010).

27. Killen, M., Sinno, S., & Margie, N. G. (2007). Children's experiences and judgments about group exclusion and inclusion. In R. V. Kail (Ed.), *Advances in child development and behavior* (pp. 173–218). New York: Elsevier.

28. Killen & Rutland. (2011).

29. Killen et al. (2007).

30. Horn, S. S., Szalacha, L. A., & Drill, K. (2008). Schooling, sexuality, and rights: An investigation of heterosexual students' social cognition regarding sexual orientation and the rights of gay and lesbian peers in school. *Journal of Social Issues*, *64*(4), 791–813. doi:10.1111/j.1540-4560.2008.00589.x

31. Møller, S. J., & Tenenbaum, H. R. (2011). Danish majority children's reasoning about exclusion based on gender and ethnicity. *Child Development*, *82*, 520–532. doi:10.1111/j.1467-8624.2010.01568.x

32. Verkuyten, M., Weesie, J., & Eijberts, M. (2011). The evaluation of perpetrators and victims of peer victimization: An extended crossed-categorization approach. *European Journal of Social Psychology*, *41*, 324–334. doi:10.1002/ejsp.777

33. Malti et al. (2012).

34. Allport, G. W. (1954). *The nature of prejudice*. Reading, MA: Addison-Wesley; Brown, R., & Hewstone, M. (2005). An integrative theory of intergroup contact. In M. P. Zanna (Ed.), *Advances in experimental social psychology* (Vol. 37, pp. 255–343). New York: Elsevier Academic Press; Pettigrew, T. F., & Tropp, L. R. (2006). A meta-analytic test of intergroup contact theory. *Journal of Personality and Social Psychology*, *90*(5), 751–783. doi:10.1037/0022-3514.90.5.751

35. Nesdale, D., Maass, A., Durkin, K., & Griffiths, J. (2005). Group norms, threat, and children's racial prejudice. *Child Development*, *76*(3), 652–663.

36. Rutland et al. (2010).

37. Turiel. (2002).

38. Killen, M., Rutland, A., Abrams, D., Mulvey, K. L., & Hitti, A. (2012). Development of intra- and intergroup judgments in the context of moral and social-conventional norms. *Child Development*.

39. Hitti, A., Mulvey, K. L., Rutland, A., Abrams, D., & Killen, M. (2012). Excluding group members who challenge moral and social-conventional group norms: Children's and adolescents' reasoning and affective evaluations. Manuscript submitted for publication.

40. Hitti et al. (2012).

41. Turiel, E. (2002); Killen & Rutland. (2011).

SHELBY COOLEY *is a doctoral student in developmental science in the Department of Human Development and Quantitative Methodology at the University of Maryland, College Park.*

LAURA ELENBAAS *is a doctoral student in developmental science in the Department of Human Development and Quantitative Methodology at the University of Maryland, College Park.*

MELANIE KILLEN *is a professor of human development and quantitative methodology and associate director of the Center for Children, Relationships, and Culture at the University of Maryland, College Park.*

Why do the emotions children and adolescents anticipate in the context of (im)moral actions predict actual behavior? It is argued that these emotions reflect different forms of moral agency that emerge in the course of children's and adolescents' moral development.

4

Linking moral emotion attributions with behavior: Why "(un)happy victimizers" and "(un)happy moralists" act the way they feel

Tobias Krettenauer

YOUNG CHILDREN AROUND the age of four years perfectly know that stealing a candy bar from a classmate or pushing another child off a swing is wrong because of the harm that is done to the victim. Still, if children at this age are asked how they would feel if they did something similar they typically report happy feelings with little appreciation of the fact that a moral rule was transgressed. This response pattern has been dubbed "happy-victimizer" attribution. Happy-victimizer responses are quite common in four- to five-year-old children and gradually decrease with age. Happy-victimizer research has demonstrated repeatedly that the emotions children and adolescents attribute in hypothetical scenarios are associated with actual (im)moral behavior.[1] A recent meta-analysis that summarized over forty experimental and correlational studies with more than eight thousand participants ages four to twenty years reported a significant relationship between children's and adolescents' moral emotion attributions and social behavior.[2] This association was strongest for antisocial behavior and emotions attributed to the self, with an effect size of d = .49. Thus, the emotions children and adolescents anticipate for themselves in the context of moral transgressions clearly have implications for their behavioral conduct. Strikingly, in this meta-analysis, the association between moral emotion attributions and behavior was not moderated by participants' age. Thus, the relationship between moral emotion attributions and social behavior was not limited to a specific developmental period.

Why do the emotions children and adolescents anticipate in the context of hypothetical scenarios predict their actual behavior in various social settings and across a broad age range? This is the leading question of this article. I first discuss a common and initially plausible answer to this question that provides a motivational account of moral emotion attributions. According to this view, moral emotion attributions reflect the development of moral motivation. The discussion of this view, however, will lead to an important qualification of the leading question: moral emotion attributions do not necessarily reflect actual emotional experiences in the context of (im)moral actions but should be more appropriately viewed as cognitive representations of emotional experiences related to future (im)moral actions. I describe three ways in which these cognitive representations are linked with children's and adolescents' decision making and behavior. These links correspond to three layers in the development of moral selfhood that I outline at the end of the article. It is suggested that moral emotion attributions are linked with moral behavior because they exemplify different forms of moral selfhood or moral agency that emerge in the course of children's and adolescents' development.

The motivational account and its limitations

A common answer to the question of why moral emotion attributions predict actual behavior relates to moral motivation. It is assumed that children's moral emotion attributions predict behavior because they reflect moral motivation. This idea rests on a functionalist understanding of moral emotions, according to which emotions signal those aspects of the person-environment relationship that are of particular importance and worth acting on.[3] It has been most strongly promoted by Nunner-Winkler, who distinguished two major phases in moral development.[4] First, children come to learn moral rules in an informational sense. They know what is morally right and wrong but do not attach any personal significance to this knowledge. In the second phase, as they gradually internalize and integrate moral knowledge into the self, children develop a "second-order desire" for doing what they consider morally right. Whereas the acquisition of moral knowledge is described as a general process that applies to all children in roughly the same way, development of moral motivation is considered multidirectional. Some children gain moral motivation in the course of development, and others lose it. As a consequence, individual differences in moral motivation tend to persist well beyond childhood. As Nunner-Winkler put it, "Moral development is a two-layered process: The first step is the early and universal acquisition of moral knowledge, the second step is the slow and hard process of building up moral motivation."[5] In this model, the development of moral motivation is considered largely independent of the development of moral cognition. Moral motivation is thus noncognitive. The model is meant to explain both the increase in moral emotions attributions in the childhood years and consistent association between moral emotion attributions and moral behavior across ages.

At first glance, this motivational explanation for why moral emotion attributions predict actual behavior seems plausible. However, a closer look renders it problematic. There is unequivocal empirical evidence that children engage in prosocial and moral actions well before they start to attribute feelings of guilt or shame to a moral wrongdoer in hypothetical scenarios around the age of seven or eight years.[6] Children at the age of two years spontaneously help a stranger without expecting a benefit in return.[7] Thus, they are motivated to act morally well before they acquire moral motivation in Nunner-Winkler's account. In a similar vein, children express moral emotions of guilt or shame in their nonverbal behavior at the age of four or five years, well before these emotions show up in corresponding emotion attributions.[8] Thus, if moral emotions are an indicator of moral motivation, children are morally motivated well before they anticipate moral emotions in hypothetical scenarios.

One might object at this point that moral emotion attributions as assessed in happy-victimizer research may reflect a specific type of moral motivation that is not present in two year olds but emerges later in the course of development. This form of motivation has been described by Nunner-Winkler as a second-order desire for doing what a person considers right in a particular situation.[9] Second-order desires are desires about desires (e.g., the desire not to selfishly desire everything for oneself). Such desires are hardly independent of the development of moral reasoning capabilities. The notion of moral motivation as a second-order desire thus conflicts with the idea of moral development as a two-layered process where the acquisition of moral motivation is independent of moral reasoning development.[10] Moreover, Malti and colleagues did not find any effect of moral emotion attributions as a predictor of prosocial behavior that was independent of sympathy.[11] Thus, the idea that moral emotion attributions reflect a distinct type of moral motivation has not been supported by empirical research so far.

Criticizing the motivational account of moral emotion attributions does not deny that these attributions predict social behavior. The question is how to make sense of this finding. Why do the emotions children and adolescents anticipate in the context of hypothetical scenarios predict their actual behavior? Any reference to moral motivation as an independent factor that accounts for this predictive relationship is problematic. The motivational account explains the motivational significance of moral emotion attributions by referring to moral motivation. It is, thus, at the verge of being circular. Moreover, it does not clearly enough differentiate between the moral emotions children and adolescents actually experience in the wake of (im)moral behavior and the cognitive representations they develop about these emotional experiences. These two aspects—the actual experience of emotions on the one hand and the cognitive representations about emotional experiences on the other—are not just two sides of the same coin. Although cognitive representations of emotions may be based on past emotional experiences, building cognitive representations about experiences is always an active and (re)constructive process in which memories about the past are (re)shaped and transformed by current concerns. Research about autobiographical memories is full of rich examples for such a constructive process.[12] Moreover, cognitive representations about moral emotions can be about emotional experiences individuals have never before experienced. If this were not the case, it would be impossible to investigate emotional responses to hypothetical situations that are unlikely to happen in people's lives. In these situations, the constructive nature of emotion attributions is clearly dominant.

As is well documented in the social psychological literature on affective forecasting, individuals often overestimate the intensity and duration of their emotional reactions to possible future events.[13] This overestimation might be advantageous: it might serve as a motivator to obtain things that are anticipated to have positive emotional consequences as well as to avoid situations that are expected to have negative consequences. Children's moral emotion attributions are no exception to this general tendency. Smith found that three- to eight-year-old children who predicted not sharing with another child in an experiment overestimated their negative feelings about sharing as compared to the actual emotional experience of sharing, which was more positive.[14] Thus, the emotions children anticipated for not sharing seemed to be more predictive for their decision making than the actual emo-

NEW DIRECTIONS FOR YOUTH DEVELOPMENT • DOI: 10.1002/yd

tional experience. From this perspective, the question of how to account for the relationship between moral emotion attributions and behavior turns into the question of how cognitively constructed representations of emotional experiences related to future (im)moral behavior are linked with children's and adolescents' decision making and action. This is the question the remainder of the article focuses on.

Links between moral emotion attributions, decision making, and action

It is likely that the theoretical link between moral emotion attributions is not constant over the course of development; many parameters play a role in this context, such as children's theory of mind, emotion understanding, judgment, and decision making, and are subject to developmental change. However, this assumption stands in stark contrast to the empirical finding of a consistent relationship between moral emotion attributions and social behavior that was not moderated by age.[15] This constant empirical relationship suggests that depending on age, different mechanisms are at work that link moral emotion attributions with behavior.

I propose three links that connect moral emotion attributions with behavior. Moral emotions attributions may reflect a dominant desire (link 1), or they may represent outcome expectancies (link 2) or an emotional response to anticipated (in)consistencies of the self (link 3).

Dominant desire: Link 1

There is no question that children around the age of two years, well before they develop a theory of mind, understand the emotional implications of fulfilling a desire or frustrating it.[16] If you get what you desire, you feel happy; if not, you feel sad. Consequently, you do not want to feel sad because this would be equivalent to not wanting what you desire. At a very young age, there is a clear con-

NEW DIRECTIONS FOR YOUTH DEVELOPMENT • DOI: 10.1002/yd

nection between intentional states and emotions. Emotions indicate an intentional state (desire). If this finding is transferred to emotion attributions in the context of (im)moral actions, it can be assumed that the emotions children anticipate in this context reflect intentional states. For example, if you feel good about pushing another girl, you want to push her; if you feel bad about it, you do not want to push her. In other words, emotion attributions signal a dominant desire. This is the most direct link between emotion attributions and behavior that likely is established around the age of two years.

Outcome expectancies: Link 2

Whereas young children clearly understand the relation between emotions and intentional states such as desires, their emotion understanding is still limited in important respects. Children up to the age of seven or eight years have single representations of discrete emotions (for example, happy, sad, or mad) but are not able to integrate representational sets for positive and negative emotions.[17] Correspondingly, young children do not understand mixed emotions. They deny that two opposite feelings can simultaneously coexist.[18] As a consequence, they are unable to understand that a moral transgression may cause both positive and negative emotions at the same time. It is typically not until the age of seven or eight years that children understand that a moral transgression may lead to both positive and negative emotions: positive emotions because the child achieved what she or he wanted and negative emotions because a rule was transgressed.[19] Once this understanding is established, the way emotion attributions relate to decision making and action changes fundamentally: moral emotions become part of a larger set of outcome expectancies. In this larger context of outcome expectancies, negative self-evaluative emotions such as guilt feelings count as costs that make a moral transgression less likely. These favorable and unfavorable consequences of an action need to be considered when making a moral decision.

Thus, different from the direct link where moral emotion attributions signal a dominant desire, moral emotion attributions reflect outcomes the child needs to consider in a decision-making process. This view is consistent with the social information processing approach that has been quite successful in predicting children's and adolescents' social behavior.[20]

Emotional response to anticipated (in)consistencies of the self: Link 3

From an information processing view, moral actions follow the same logic as any other instrumental action: individuals want to maximize benefits and minimize costs. This logic is characteristic of stage 2 reasoning in Kohlberg's model and describes the way children at the preconventional level of moral reasoning approach situations where morality and self-interest conflict. However, as children move into stage 3, they start to consider these situations from a third-person perspective, where a moral decision needs to be justifiable on the grounds of shared normative expectations about what is morally right in a given situation. Once this level is achieved, moral emotion attributions signal an emotional response related to shared normative beliefs that the individual accepts as valid and important.[21] Thus, moral emotion attributions reflect normative feelings rather than mere factual outcome expectancies. Blasi described these normative feelings aptly as "expressive in nature." They are "not seen as a self-punishing response or as signal anxiety whose function is to prevent future misbehavior." Rather, guilt is seen as "an emotional response to the perception of a serious fracture in one's self, analogous to the cry of pain when the body is wounded or when a loved one is lost."[22] Thus, once children have transcended immediate self-interest as the guiding principle for moral decision making (stage 2), attributions of moral emotions start to reflect a desire for self-consistency.

To summarize up to this point, moral emotion attributions were defined as cognitive representations of emotional experiences related to future (im)moral actions. These representations are linked to actual decision making and behavior in three ways: they can signal a dominant desire (link 1), represent outcome expectancies (link 2), or reflect an emotional response to anticipated (in)consistencies of the self (link 3). These three links vary with regard to psychological complexity and describe a developmental sequence. Link 1 emerges first in the course of development, followed by link 2, which eventually leads to link 3. Although there is a clear developmental order, the three links do not describe hierarchical stages in a Kohlbergian sense. Link 2 does not replace link 1, and link 3 does not supersede link 2. In normally developing adolescents, all three links coexist.

Moral emotion attributions and the developing moral self

It has been often argued that moral emotion attributions represent individuals' moral self or moral identity and that this self-relevance of emotion attributions ultimately accounts for their motivational relevance.[23] Tracy and Robins maintained that standards, rules, and goals need to be considered relevant to one's identity to elicit self-evaluative emotions.[24] In line with this assumption, significant correlations between the self-importance of moral values and moral emotion attributions were reported in various samples of adolescents.[25] Moreover, Johnston and Krettenauer found that moral emotion attributions mediate the link between the self-importance of moral values and adolescents' delinquent behavior.[26] Although this research provides evidence to support proposed link 3, it leaves the correlation between moral emotion attributions and behavior that was found in childhood unaccounted for.

Advocates of the self model in moral psychology typically maintain that self and morality are two developmental systems that are largely unconnected in childhood but become gradually integrated in the course of adolescent development. It is thus the presumed integration of moral values into the adolescent self-concept that gives rise to a moral self—a self that profoundly cares about matters of morality and ethical conduct. Once a moral self is established in adolescence, emotion attributions are linked with behavior as anticipated emotional reactions to (in)consistencies within the self (link 3). Following this view, the proposed links 1 and 2 would not involve a moral self. However, the fact that emotion attributions effectively predict children's behavior suggests otherwise. Thus, a moral self might be established much earlier than commonly assumed. The well-documented finding that moral emotion attributions predict children's social behavior in conjunction with this attempt to account for this relationship on a theoretical level urges us to reconsider common models of moral self-development. This is an important theoretical implication that I present and address at the end of the article.

A three-layer model of moral self-development

The proposed links between moral emotion attributions and children's and adolescents' social behavior correspond to a three-layer model of moral self-development.[27] This model differentiates three conceptions of moral agency: the self as (1) intentional, (2) volitional, and (3) identified agent. Once children are able to carry moral intentions, they have developed a moral self at the level of intentional actions.

There is little doubt that children at the age of two years already spontaneously engage in prosocial actions of helping, sharing, and caring without expecting a benefit in return. They actively want to promote others' well-being and avoid inflicting harm on them, at least occasionally. When this situation occurs, a moral self on the level of intentional action is established. However, at that young age, children are regularly overpowered by emotions of anger or envy, leading to acts of instrumental or retaliatory aggression. Often their egoistic desires prevail. Children need to develop the ability to regulate egoistic desires and resist antisocial impulses, that is, prioritize moral desires over competing desires.

NEW DIRECTIONS FOR YOUTH DEVELOPMENT • DOI: 10.1002/yd

Once they have developed this ability, a volitional moral self is established.

In an earlier developmental phase, this volitional self may be largely based on considerations external to the self, such as fear of retribution or punishment. A fully integrated sense of self requires that the individual experiences the act of prioritizing a moral desire over an immoral desire as a volition that emanates from the self rather than as a decision that is imposed by external factors. In other words, shoulds need to be transformed into wants. Various models of self, ego, and identity development propose a general developmental trend toward higher levels of self-integration. These models generally assume that individuals' commitments to values and ideals are increasingly experienced as self-chosen rather than imposed by external factors.[28] Even Kohlberg's stage model of moral development evidences a decline of external regulation as teenagers move out of preconventional stages 1 and 2 and standards of individual conscience become more salient at stages 3 and 4.[29] Once a child or teenager prioritizes moral desires over egoistic desires and feels that this prioritization reflects the way she or he wants to be, the volitional self has turned into an identified agent.

The self as an intentional agent is foundational for the self as a volitional agent, and the volitional self is foundational for the self as identified agent. However, this relationship does not imply levels or stages. Thus, the self as intentional agent is not replaced by the volitional self, and the volitional self is not superseded by the self as identified agent. All three forms of moral selfhood coexist, similar to the links between moral emotion attributions and behavior described above (for an illustration of this model, see Figure 4.1). Moral emotion attributions that reflect a dominant desire (link 1) are an instantiation of the moral self as intentional agent. When moral emotion attributions represent different outcome expectancies that need to be considered in the decision-making process (link 2), they require a volitional self. Finally, moral emotion attributions that reflect an emotional response to (in)consistencies within the self (link 3) describe a moral agent who identifies himself or herself with moral values. Thus, link 3 requires value

Figure 4.1. Three layers of moral self-development and the corresponding links between moral emotion attributions and behavior

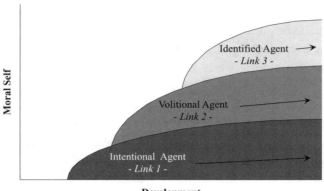

identifications. From this perspective, the three proposed links that connect moral emotion attributions with children's and adolescents' actual behavior are not limited to moral emotions and their cognitive representations. Rather, they exemplify different forms of moral agency that emerge in the course of children's and adolescents' development.

Conclusion

This article started with a critique of the view that moral emotion attributions are a direct outgrowth of the development of moral motivation. It has finished with the proposal that moral emotion attributions are linked to moral behavior because they exemplify different forms of moral agency that emerge in the course of children's and adolescents' development. Both statements may sound vexingly similar. It may therefore be helpful to point out the difference between these two positions as a way to summarize my major points.

According to the motivational account of moral emotion attributions that Nunner-Winkler promoted, moral motivation is a single developmental dimension that is fully separable from moral judgment and thus noncognitive. I have provided a different picture. According to this view, moral motivation is complex and heterogeneous. Different processes are at work that lead to moral action. From the perspective of an agentic self, these processes relate to spontaneous moral desires, moral volitions, and value identifications. All processes are intimately tied to moral reasoning and decision making.

The view that moral motivation accounts for moral emotion attributions is overly simplistic. Moral emotion attributions are motivationally relevant. However, this motivational relevance should be viewed as the explanandum rather than the explanans of moral emotion attributions. Thus, moral emotion attributions create motivation to act rather than depend on it. This article should be understood as an attempt to clarify the motivating role that moral emotion attributions play in children's and adolescents' moral development.

Notes

1. Asendorpf, J. B., & Nunner-Winkler, G. (1992). Children's moral motive strength and temperamental inhibition reduce their immoral behavior in real moral conflicts. *Child Development, 63,* 1223–1235; Lake, N., Lane, S., & Harris, P. L. (1995). The expectation of guilt and resistance to temptation. *Early Development and Parenting, 4,* 63–73; Malti, T., Gummerum, M., Keller, M., & Buchmann, M. (2009). Children's moral motivation, sympathy, and prosocial behavior. *Child Development, 80,* 442–460.

2. Malti, T., & Krettenauer, T. (2012). The relation of moral emotion attributions to pro- and antisocial behavior: A meta-analysis. *Child Development.* Advance online publication. 10.1111/j.1467-8624.2012.01851.x

3. See Krettenauer, T., Malti, T., & Sokol, B. W. (2008). Development of moral emotions and the happy-victimizer phenomenon: A critical review of theory and application. *European Journal of Developmental Science, 2,* 221–235.

4. Nunner-Winkler, G. (1999). Development of moral understanding and moral motivation. In F. E. Weinert & W. Schneider (Eds.), *Individual development from 3 to 12* (pp. 253–292). Cambridge: Cambridge University Press; Nunner-Winkler, G. (2007). Development of moral motivation from childhood to early adulthood. *Journal of Moral Education, 36,* 399–414; Nunner-Winkler, G. (2009). Moral motivation from childhood to early adulthood. In W. Schneider & M. Bullock (Eds.), *Human development from early childhood to early adulthood* (pp. 91–118). New York, NY: Psychology Press.

5. Nunner-Winkler, G. (1993). Die Entwicklung moralischer Motivation. In W. Edelstein, G. Nunner-Winkler, & G. Noam (Eds.), *Moral und Person* (pp. 278–303). Frankfurt am Main: Suhrkamp. P. 281.

6. See Dunfield, K., Kuhlmeier, V. A., O'Connell, L., & Kelley, E. (2011). Examining the diversity of prosocial behavior: Helping, sharing, and comforting in infancy. *Infancy, 16*, 227–247; Svetlova, M., Nichols, S. R., & Brownell, C. A. (2010). Toddlers' prosocial behavior: From instrumental to empathic to altruistic helping. *Child Development, 81*, 1814–1827.

7. Warneken, F., & Tomasello, M. (2009). The roots of human altruism. *British Journal of Psychology, 100*, 455–471. doi:10.1348/000712608X379061

8. Kochanska, G., & Aksan, N. (2006). Children's conscience and self-regulation. *Journal of Personality, 76*, 1587–1617.

9. See also Blasi, A. (2005). Moral character: A psychological approach. In D. K. Lapsley & F. C. Power (Eds.), *Character psychology and character education* (pp. 67–100). Notre Dame, IN: University of Notre Dame Press.

10. Minnameier, G. (2010). The problem of moral motivation and the happy victimizer phenomenon: Killing two birds with one stone. In B. Latzko & T. Malti (Eds.), *Children's moral emotions and moral cognition: Developmental and educational perspectives* (pp. 55–75). San Francisco, CA: Jossey-Bass.

11. Malti, T., Gummerum, M., Keller, M., & Buchmann, M. (2009). Children's moral motivation, sympathy, and prosocial behavior. *Child Development, 80*, 442–460.

12. Wilson, A. E., & Ross, M. (2003). The identity function of autobiographical memory: Time is on our side. *Memory, 11*, 137–149; Krettenauer, T., & Mosleh, M. (in press). Remembering your (im)moral past: Autobiographical reasoning and moral identity development. *Identity: An International Journal of Theory and Research.*

13. Wilson, T. D., & Gilbert, D. T. (2005). Affective forecasting. *Current Directions in Psychological Science, 14*, 131–134.

14. Smith, C. E. (2010, June). *Children's affective forecasts in the context of sharing.* Paper presented at the Annual Meeting of the Jean Piaget Society, St. Louis, MO.

15. Malti, T., & Krettenauer, T. (2012). The relation of moral emotion attributions to pro- and antisocial behavior: A meta-analysis. *Child Development.* Advance online publication. 10.1111/j.1467-8624.2012.01851.x

16. Wellman, H. M., & Phillips, A. T. (2001). Developing intentional understandings. In B. F. Malle, L. J. Moses, & D. A. Baldwin (Eds.), *Intentions and intentionality* (pp. 125–148). Cambridge, MA: MIT Press.

17. Mascolo, M. F., & Fischer, K. W. (1995). Developmental transformations in appraisals for pride, shame, and guilt. In J. P. Tangney & K. W. Fischer (Eds.), *Self-conscious emotions: The psychology of shame, guilt, embarrassment and pride* (pp. 64–113). New York, NY: Guilford Press.

18. Harter, S., & Whitesell, N. R. (1989). Developmental changes in children's understanding of single, multiple, and blended emotion concepts. In C. Saarni & P. L. Harris (Eds.), *Children's understanding of emotions* (pp. 81–116). Cambridge: Cambridge University Press.

19. Arsenio, W. F., & Kramer, R. (1992). Victimizers and their victims: Children's conceptions of the mixed emotional consequences of moral transgressions. *Child Development, 63,* 915–927.
20. Coie, J. D., & Dodge, K. A. (1998). Aggression and antisocial behavior. In W. Damon (Ed.), *Handbook of child psychology* (Vol. 3, pp. 779–862). Hoboken, NJ: Wiley.
21. Keller, M., Brandt, A., & Sigurdardottir, G. (2010). "Happy" and "unhappy" victimizers: The development of moral emotions from childhood to adolescence. In W. Koops, D. Brugman, T. J. Ferguson, & A. F. Sanders (Eds.), *The development and structure of conscience* (pp. 253–268). Hove, UK: Psychology Press.
22. Blasi, A. (1983). Moral cognition and moral action: A theoretical perspective. *Developmental Review, 3,* 178–210. P. 204.
23. Blasi, A. (1999). Emotions and moral motivation. *Journal for the Theory of Social Behavior, 29,* 1–19; Krettenauer, T., Malti, T., & Sokol, B. W. (2008). Development of moral emotions and the happy-victimizer phenomenon: A critical review of theory and application. *European Journal of Developmental Science, 2,* 221–235; Mascolo, M. F., & Fischer, K. W. (2007). The codevelopment of self and sociomoral emotions during the toddler years. In C. A. Brownell & C. B. Kopp (Eds.), *Socioemotional development in the toddler years* (pp. 66–99). New York, NY: Guilford Press; Keller, M., Brandt, A., & Sigurdardottir, G. (2010). "Happy" and "unhappy" victimizers: The development of moral emotions from childhood to adolescence. In W. Koops, D. Brugman, T. J. Ferguson, & A. F. Sanders (Eds.), *The development and structure of conscience* (pp. 253–268). Hove, UK: Psychology Press.
24. Tracy, J., & Robins, R. W. (2004). Putting the self into self-conscious emotions: A theoretical model. *Psychological Inquiry, 15,* 103–125.
25. Krettenauer, T. (2011). The dual moral self: Moral centrality and intrinsic moral motivation. *Journal of Genetic Psychology, 172,* 309–328. doi:10.1080/00221325.2010.538451; Nunner-Winkler, G., Meyer-Nikele, M., & Wohlrab, D. (2007). Gender differences in moral motivation. *Merrill-Palmer Quarterly, 53,* 26–52.
26. Johnston, M., & Krettenauer, T. (2011). Moral self and moral emotion expectancies as predictors of anti- and prosocial behavior in adolescence: A case for mediation? *European Journal of Developmental Psychology, 8,* 228–243. doi:10.1080/17405621003619945
27. This model is described in Krettenauer, T. (in press-a). Moral motivation, responsibility and the development of the moral self. In K. Heinrichs & F. Oser (Eds.), *Handbook of moral motivation: What makes people act morally?* Rotterdam: Sense Publishers; Krettenauer, T. (in press-b). Revisiting the moral self construct: Developmental perspectives on moral selfhood. In B. Sokol, U. F. Grouzet, & U. Müller (Eds.), *Self-regulation and autonomy.* Cambridge: Cambridge University Press.
28. Blasi, A., & Glodis, K. (1995). The development of identity. A critical analysis from the perspective of the self as subject. *Developmental Review, 15,* 404–433; Loevinger, J. (1976). *Ego development.* San Francisco, CA: Jossey-Bass; Marcia, J. E., Waterman, A. S., Matteson, D. R., Archer, S. L., & Orlof-

sky, J. L. (1993). *Ego identity.* New York, NY: Springer-Verlag; Deci, E. L., & Ryan, R. M. (1991). A motivational approach to self: Integration in personality. In R. Dienstbier (Ed.), *Nebraska Symposium on motivation, Vol. 38. Perspectives on motivation* (pp. 237–288). Lincoln: University of Nebraska Press.

29. Gibbs, J. C., Basinger, K. S., & Fuller, D. (1992). *Moral maturity: Measuring the development of sociomoral reflection.* Mahwah, NJ: Erlbaum.

TOBIAS KRETTENAUER *is an associate professor for developmental psychology at Wilfrid Laurier University, Ontario, Canada.*

The chapter focuses on the relative contributions of guilt, shame, and sympathy in predicting prosocial and aggressive behaviors.

5

Behaving badly or goodly: Is it because I feel guilty, shameful, or sympathetic? Or is it a matter of what I think?

Gustavo Carlo, Meredith McGinley,
Alexandra Davis, Cara Streit

THE PRIMACY OF cognitions versus emotions in understanding moral development has become a resurgent area of debate and scholarship. Early theorists of moral psychology emphasized the role of cognitive processes, such as moral reasoning and perspective taking, as reflective of moral standing.[1] whereas other scholars proposed a more central role of moral emotions, such as sympathy, guilt, and shame.[2] Despite the debate on the centrality of these processes, scholars acknowledged that both cognitive and emotive processes can play important roles in morality.[3] However, recently, strong claims place emotion-based, intuitive processes as most informative relative to cognitive processes.[4] Unfortunately, these provocative claims contradict the large body of evidence that demonstrates the dual-central roles of moral cognitions and

NEW DIRECTIONS FOR YOUTH DEVELOPMENT, NO. 136, WINTER 2012 © WILEY PERIODICALS, INC.
Published online in Wiley Online Library (wileyonlinelibrary.com) • DOI: 10.1002/yd.20040

emotions and steer the field away from the recent advances in moral scholarship.

Traditional approaches to moral development

Since Piaget's early scholarly work on moral development, cognitive-developmental researchers have advanced the discipline considerably.[5] Led by the sophisticated theoretical tenets of Kohlberg's theory, these researchers demonstrated the central role of socio-cognitive processes such as perspective taking in the gradual maturation of moral reasoning across childhood and adolescence.[6] Although early cognitive developmentalists were less interested in the role of emotions, there were opportunities for emotive-based processes to inform cognitive-developmental processes. Indeed, some revisionist theorists integrated emotion-based processes into cognitive-developmental theory.[7] In recent years, the central role of cognitive processes has been extended by social information processing theorists and social cognitive theorists.[8]

Other notable scholars conducted extensive research on moral emotions during this early period.[9] One of the best-known and early advocates of the role of emotive-based processes in moral development was Martin Hoffman.[10] Based on the philosophic writings of Hume and Blum, Hoffman proposed that both socio-cognitive and socioemotive processes are coexisting sources of influence in moral development.[11] For example, perspective taking helps foster empathic distress (or sympathy) responding. Moreover, empathy and sympathy are important predictors of prosocial and moral behaviors. Several other prominent scholars extended Hoffman's theory, which spurred substantial research on the importance of socioemotions such as empathy, sympathy, guilt, and shame.[12]

Recent research on morality (due in part to advances in biomedical methods) has led to several exciting discoveries.[13] For example, there is mounting evidence of the coexisting interplay of neural activity in regions of the brain that are associated with both cognitive and emotive processing during moral decision making and actions.[14] Furthermore, experimental manipulation and longitudinal studies show that both emotive- and cognitive-based processes are predictive of moral behaviors across the life span.[15] Indeed, the questions regarding the role of moral cognitions and emotions have shifted to understanding the interplay of such processes rather than the relative importance of one over the other.[16] Consequently, there is extensive interest in comprehensive moral theories (for example, moral identity, social cognitive) that integrate sociocognitive and socioemotive mechanisms.[17]

Toward an integrative understanding of morality

This article is based on the premise that accounting for both sociocognitive and socioemotive processes will better explain moral behaviors. We tested two models that highlight the interplay of guilt, shame, sympathy, perspective taking, and prosocial moral reasoning in predicting prosocial and aggressive behaviors.

Guilt, Shame, and Moral Behaviors

Several scholars have proposed that guilt, an aversive feeling resulting from a failure to meet one's personal moral standard, can serve to motivate moral behaviors.[18] In contrast, shame, which refers to belittling one's self as a result of failing to meet other people's moral standards, is considered debilitating to moral functioning. While most individuals are prone to both guilt and shame, there are individual differences in these tendencies.[19] However, scholars have noted that moral emotions can be induced or primed by moral cognitions, and vice versa.[20] For example, failing to meet one's personal moral standards might induce higher-level moral reasoning regarding the other's situation. Alternatively, thinking about the moral situation of another person who has been wronged by the individual could induce or reduce feelings of guilt. Over time, these event-specific situations could develop into tendencies that are automatically enacted in similar, future moral situations.[21]

Despite the conceptual links among guilt and shame and moral cognitions and behaviors, sparse research exists. Prior research shows relatively consistent positive associations between guilt and positive moral development outcomes.[22] However, research on shame is mixed. In studies of European American college students, shame is negatively linked to moral development.[23] In contrast, in studies of early adolescents and in Asian culture groups, shame is positively linked to moral development.[24] These researchers have suggested that shame might be positively related to moral development if the shame is not personalized or integrated into one's moral self-concept. Surprisingly, research on the links between guilt and shame and moral reasoning is sparse.

Sympathy, Moral Reasoning, and Moral Behaviors

However, there has been substantial research on the links between sympathy and moral behaviors. Conceptually, sympathy, or feelings of sorrow or concern for others, is often considered the basis for altruistic and other forms of prosocial behaviors (actions that benefit others).[25] Moreover, sympathy requires perspective taking (understanding another's situation).[26] The notion is that feelings of sympathy orient individuals toward the needs of others and inhibit the urge to harm or injure others. Both sympathy and perspective taking are empirically positively linked to prosocial behaviors and negatively linked to aggression.[27] Furthermore, perspective taking and sympathy are interrelated.[28]

Moral reasoning has also been linked to moral development. Although the bulk of such research has focused on prohibitive reasoning, moral reasoning regarding laws or social rules, recent work has emphasized prosocial (or care-based) moral reasoning.[29] Prosocial moral reasoning involves thinking when presented with an opportunity to help another in the relative absence of formal laws or social rules.[30] Eisenberg has demonstrated age-related increases in prosocial moral reasoning from early-appearing hedonistic, approval-oriented, and needs-oriented modes to later-emerging other-oriented, stereotyped (stereotyped notions of what is "good"), and (empathic) internalized modes.[31] As such, prosocial moral reasoning is strongly linked conceptually to both prosocial and aggressive behaviors, and research findings support these conceptual links.[32] Because moral emotions can induce moral reasoning, one might also expect that sympathy and guilt might induce higher-level and other-oriented forms of prosocial moral reasoning, which in turn might predict moral behaviors. Therefore, we also examined the mediating role of prosocial moral reasoning in the relations between moral emotions and behaviors.

Multidimensionality of Moral Behaviors

Another recent research advance is to examine specific forms of moral behaviors. Based on prior theory and research, Carlo and Randall identified six broad types of prosocial behaviors (or tendencies).[33] Altruistic behaviors refer to the tendency to help without expectation for self-reward. Helping in front of others is referred to as public prosocial behaviors. Helping others who request assistance is deemed compliant prosocial behaviors. Anonymous prosocial behaviors reflect helping others without their knowledge. Dire prosocial behaviors occur in crisis or emergency situations, and emotional prosocial behaviors are expressed in affectively evocative contexts. Evidence is accumulating on the distinction among these six types of prosocial tendencies and specific correlates of these constructs.[34]

Based primarily on prior research with European American college students, guilt was expected to induce higher levels of prosocial moral reasoning and, in turn, higher levels of prosocial behaviors and lower levels of aggressive behaviors.

In contrast, shame was not (or perhaps was negatively) expected to be significantly associated with prosocial moral reasoning, and perhaps negatively related to prosocial behaviors and positively related to aggression. We deemed this the *guilt-based model.*

The *sympathy-based model* suggests that perspective taking positively predicts sympathy and prosocial moral reasoning. In turn, prosocial moral reasoning ought to be positively related to prosocial behaviors and negatively related to aggression. In addition, perspective taking and sympathy should be positively associated with prosocial behaviors but negatively associated with aggression.

Because research on the six types of prosocial behaviors is rare, predictions of specific forms of prosocial behavior were exploratory. Finally, we also explored whether the models differed for men and women.

Method

Participants and procedure

The participants were 207 undergraduate college students (48 percent male, M age = 20.04, SD = 2.55) from a public university in the Midwest. The survey packet was completed in small groups in a quiet classroom, and students received course credit for participating.

Materials

Prosocial tendencies measure. Participants completed the Prosocial Tendencies Measure-Revised (PTM-R) to assess their tendency to engage in helping behaviors in different situations.[35] Participants rated items on a 5-point Likert scale according to how likely they are to engage in each type of behavior (1 = does not describe me at all, 5 = describes me greatly).

The PTM-R consists of six subscales: Each item is assessed on a 5-point Likert scale (1 = does not describe me at all, 5 = describes me greatly).

- Altruistic, which is helping with no gain to the self (four reverse-coded items, for example, "I tend to help with charity work best when it looks good on my résumé"; alpha = .76)
- Public, helping in the presence of others (three items, for example, "I tend to help best when people are watching me"; alpha = .83)

- Emotional, helping in emotionally evocative situations (five items, for example, "I tend to comfort people when they are upset"; alpha = .90)
- Dire, helping in a crisis (three items, for example, "I tend to help people who are in a real crisis or emergency"; alpha = .82)
- Anonymous, helping without others knowing (four items, for example, "I tend to donate money without anyone knowing"; alpha = .86)
- Compliant, helping when asked (two items, for example, "I tend to help without hesitation when people ask"; alpha = .67)

Previous research has demonstrated good reliability and validity for the PTM-R, including good test-retest reliability, convergent validity, and discriminant validity (weakly to moderately related to social desirability and prosocial moral reasoning).[36]

Prosocial moral reasoning. The PROM contains six story dilemmas in which the participant must choose between his or her own needs and the needs of another.[37] Each of the stories contains a hedonistic item (for example, "It depends how far behind Lucy will get on her school work"), a needs-oriented item (for example, "It depends how sick the other girl will get"), an approval-oriented item (for example, "It depends on whether Lucy believes her friends or parents will like what she does"), a stereotypic item (for example, "It depends whether Lucy thinks that helping is nice or not"), and an item reflecting internalized reasoning (for example, "It depends on whether Lucy would feel badly because the other person would still be ill"). Participants rate how important each of these items is when deciding to help. Proportion scores for each subscale were computed, and then a composite was created to assess the relative preference for higher-level reasoning over lower-level reasoning.[38]

Sympathy and perspective taking. Participants completed a multidimensional measure of empathy (IRI).[39] The perspective taking and empathic concern (or sympathy) subscales are seven items each, measured on a 5-point Likert scale (0 = does not describe me well, 4 = describes me very well).

Shame and guilt. Participants completed the Test of Self-Conscious Affect (TOSCA-3), a self-report measure of one's tendency to feel shame and guilt.[40] The TOSCA-3 consists of fifteen scenarios (five positive and ten negative). After each scenario, a response item indicating a feeling of shame or guilt is presented (for example, "You would feel incompetent"). The sample item represents feelings of shame because … Participants are asked to rate their likelihood of responding in a similar manner (on a range from 1 = not likely to 5 = very likely).

Data analysis plan

In order to examine the direct and indirect relations among these observed variables, path models (see Figures 5.1 and 5.2) were tested using full structural equation modeling in Mplus 6.1.[41] The bootstrap procedure (N = 1000) was implemented in Mplus 6.1 in order to determine whether the indirect effects were statistically significant.

Figure 5.1. Path model results for the sympathy-based model

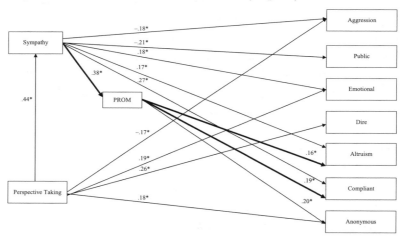

Note: PROM = prosocial moral reasoning composite. Bold lines indicate a significant indirect effect; other lines indicate a significant direct effect. Nonsignificant model paths were not depicted in the figure. Significant correlations among the outcome variables are also not depicted.

p < .05.

Figure 5.2. Path model results for the guilt-based model

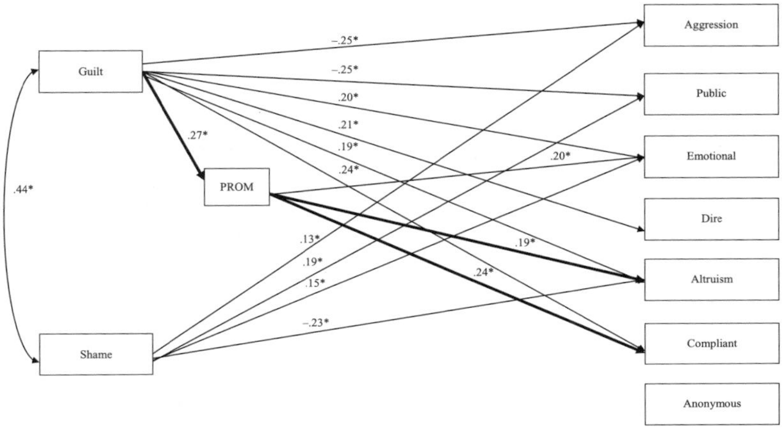

Note: PROM = prosocial moral reasoning composite. Bold lines indicate a significant indirect effect; other lines indicate a significant direct effect. Nonsignificant model paths were not depicted in the figure. Significant correlations among the outcome variables are also not depicted.

*p < .05.

Model fit in these fully constrained models was considered good if the comparative fit index (CFI) is approximately .95, or the root mean square error of approximation (RMSEA) is less than or equal to .06.[42] Model fit was examined using CFI and RMSEA in combination. In order to test gender equivalence, the models were constrained to be equal across gender. Chi-square difference tests were then conducted to examine which paths were significant across gender. All reported model parameters (i.e., path coefficients) were statistically significant at the .05 level.

Results

Mediation models

Descriptives and correlations are in Table 5.1. The sympathy-based mediation model (Figure 5.1) showed that while aggression and public prosocial behavior were negatively predicted by sympa-

Table 5.1. Descriptives and correlation matrix among the main study variables

	1	2	3	4	5	6	7	8	9	10	11	12
1. Sympathy												
2. Shame	.20*											
3. Guilt	.44*	.44*										
4. Perspective Taking	.44*	.18*	.27*									
5. PROM	.35*	.16*	.29*	.09								
6. Public	-.23*	.08	-.14*	-.08	-.16*							
7. Emotional	.31*	.26*	.30*	.29*	.22*	.08						
8. Dire	.26*	.11	.25*	.32*	.18*	.09	.64*					
9. Altruistic	.24*	-.12	.15*	.11	.23*	-.60*	-.07	-.11				
10. Compliant	.38*	.14*	.30*	.25*	.29*	-.22*	.45*	.43*	.17*			
11. Anonymous	.14*	.09	.23*	.21*	.16*	-.02	.35*	.35*	.15*	.19*		
12. Aggression	-.27*	.01	-.21*	-.25*	-.12	.23*	-.05	-.01	-.01	-.13	-.13	
Mean	3.80	32.26	44.64	2.49	.30	2.26	3.61	3.47	3.72	3.87	2.71	2.13
SD	.59	6.80	5.85	.65	.04	.88	.83	.87	.66	.86	.91	.69

Note: PROM refers to the overall prosocial moral reasoning composite. Public, emotional, dire, altruistic, compliant, and anonymous are all subscales of the prosocial tendencies measure.

$*p < .05$ level.

thy, all remaining prosocial behaviors (with the exception of dire and anonymous) were positively predicted by sympathy. Conversely, aggression was negatively predicted by perspective taking, while only emotional, dire, and anonymous prosocial behaviors were positively predicted by perspective taking. Finally, compliant and anonymous prosocial behaviors were positively predicted by prosocial moral reasoning, which in turn was positively predicted by sympathy. The standard errors for two of these three indirect effects—altruism (.001, .014) and compliant prosocial behaviors (.013, .018) fell outside zero, suggesting that prosocial moral reasoning mediated these pathways.

The guilt-based model showed that while aggression and public prosocial behaviors were negatively predicted by guilt, all remaining prosocial behaviors (with the exception of anonymous) were positively predicted by guilt. Conversely, aggression, public, and emotional prosocial behaviors were positively predicted by shame. Altruism was negatively predicted by shame. Emotional and compliant prosocial behaviors, in addition to altruism, were positively predicted by prosocial moral reasoning, which in turn was uniquely positively predicted by guilt. The standard errors for the indirect effects predicting altruism (>.000, .012) and compliant prosocial behaviors (.002, .016) fell outside the 95 percent confidence interval, suggesting that prosocial moral reasoning mediated these pathways.

Gender equivalence

The fully saturated unconstrained sympathy-based model was first estimated for both men and women ($\chi^2(0) = 0$). Next, all parameters were constrained across these two groups. The fully constrained model fit well ($\chi^2(24) = 29.963$, CFI = .99, RMSEA = .05). However the chi square difference test was not statistically significant ($p > .05$), indicating that the model did not differ across gender groups. Similarly, the fully saturated unconstrained guilt-based model was first estimated for both gender groups ($\chi^2(0) = 0$). The fully constrained model fit well ($\chi^2(24) = 23.353$, CFI = 1.00, RMSEA = .00). Again, the chi square difference test was not statistically significant ($p > .05$). Thus, the guilt-based model had equivalent fit across the gender groups.

Discussion

Overall, the findings yield supportive evidence for both sympathy- and guilt-based models of moral behaviors. Furthermore, both direct and indirect effects highlighted the role of prosocial moral reasoning in predicting such behaviors. The powerful mediating roles of prosocial moral reasoning (as well as the predictive role of perspective taking) demonstrate that moral intuitive theories are insufficient to explain moral actions. As expected, there were trait-specific relations to different types of prosocial and aggressive behaviors. Finally, there was no evidence of gender differences in the models. The findings have important implications for theories of moral development and add to the mounting evidence on the relevance of both moral emotions and moral cognitions in moral behavior.

A sympathy-based model of moral behaviors?

The sympathy-based model findings support prior conceptual models that assert the importance of sympathy as predictive of altruistic and prosocial behaviors. Specifically, sympathy positively predicted altruistic, emotional, and compliant forms of helping. However, prosocial moral reasoning also mediated the relations between sympathy and compliant and altruistic helping. These findings are consistent with the assertion that altruistic helping is more likely based on sympathy or strong internalized principles, or both.[43] In this case, the presence of both sympathy and prosocial moral reasoning increases the likelihood of selflessly motivated helping. Interestingly, prosocial moral reasoning also played a mediating role in predicting compliant helping. Thus, in essence, the interplay of moral emotions and cognitions in predicting these forms of prosocial behaviors provides additional evidence of the importance of both cognitive and emotive processes in morality.

In contrast, the findings regarding links to aggression and public helping behaviors demonstrate that sympathy, rather than prosocial moral reasoning, may better predict selfish forms of helping and aggressive behaviors. This might be due to the fact that sympathy serves to inhibit harm to others, whereas individuals may be capable of rationalizing harm to others. Therefore, moral reasoning may not be sufficient to mitigate aggression toward others. Moreover, sympathy is by definition other-oriented concern or sorrow for a needy person. Public helping appears to be motivated by a desire to gain the other's approval.[44] The inherent self-focused motives in aggressive and public behaviors seem to contradict the inherent other-focused motives in sympathy. These findings, then, suggest that the role of moral cognitions and emotions is complex and dependent on specific moral outcomes.

One other set of findings deserves mention: perspective taking was significantly and positively related to emotional, dire, and anonymous helping. These findings show support for the contention that understanding another person's situation can facilitate specific forms of helping.[45] For example, perspective taking may not predict all forms of prosocial behaviors but perhaps those forms that might require some effortful sociocognitive processing as when donating to a charitable organization, which reflects a common form of anonymous helping. Furthermore, there may be circumstances that are emergencies but the need for assistance might not be immediately obvious. For example, individuals may place themselves in dire circumstances without their own awareness. Similarly, emotionally evocative situations do not always indicate a clear need for assistance. Thus, some prosocial behaviors may require more elaborated sociocognitive processing (for example, perspective taking) to ascertain accurately whether someone is in need or how to best assist a needy person.

A guilt-based model of moral behaviors?

The guilt-based model findings also showed support for differential relations in predicting prosocial and aggressive behaviors. Guilt was positively related to compliant, altruistic, dire, and emotional helping but negatively related to public and aggressive behaviors. Similar to sympathy, prosocial moral reasoning mediated the relations between guilt and compliant and altruistic prosocial behaviors. These findings suggest that prosocial moral reasoning in combination with guilt adds to the predictive power of understanding compliant and altruistic behaviors. As before, these results provide strong evidence of the importance of prosocial moral reasoning, yielding further evidence that moral emotions are not sufficient in and of themselves to understand moral actions.

Interestingly, guilt was predictive of a wider array of prosocial behaviors than sympathy. Although sympathy is traditionally viewed as a strong motivator of moral behaviors, these findings suggest that guilt can play a major role in predicting such behaviors. Both emotions can be intrinsically driven, or they can be induced by situational factors. Furthermore, both emotions may motivate individuals to help others to avoid aversive feelings (either sorrow/sadness or uncomfortable distress), reduce suffering in others, or motivate people to live up to their own moral standards. One major difference between these moral emotions is that sympathy is vicariously induced and results from another person's needy situation.[46] Guilt, on the other hand, results from a failure to fulfill one's own moral standards to act righteously, and such ideals may apply across a wide variety of situations. Because sympathy relies on another person's needy situation, this may comparatively reduce the number of moral behaviors that sympathy may be linked to. More research to examine these relations is needed.

There were relatively few significant associations between shame and moral behaviors. However, the findings suggest that shame plays an important predictive role in selfish-based, public helping, and aggressive behaviors. Furthermore, shame negatively predicted altruistic helping behaviors. These results yield evidence that shame is linked to lower moral developmental outcomes and that it predicts selfish versus selfless forms of moral behaviors. These findings, in combination with prior research findings, suggest that despite the relatively few significant relations, shame also plays an important role in moral development.

Moral cognitions and emotions as the basis for moral actions

The overall findings underscore the need to integrate moral cognitive and emotive mechanisms into existing models of morality. There was support for both the sympathy-based and guilt-based models in predicting prosocial and aggressive behaviors. Although sympathy, guilt, and shame emotions predicted moral behaviors, there was clear evidence that moral cognitions (moral reasoning, perspective taking) played direct and indirect roles in predicting such outcomes as well. Taken together with prior evidence from experimental and longitudinal studies, the findings run contrary to notions that morality is primarily determined by emotive-based, intuitive mechanisms. Indeed, recent integrative approaches, such as social cognitive or moral identity theories, are providing richer descriptions of morality that seem to better capture the nuanced complexities of this domain.[47] Interestingly, sympathy and guilt played similar roles in predicting moral behaviors, though guilt predicted relatively more prosocial behaviors than sympathy. In contrast, shame and perspective taking predicted relatively few forms of moral behaviors. Finally, the role of cognitions and emotions was similar across men and women despite existing gender differences in such variables.

It is important not to underestimate the fact that the predictive relations were dependent on the specific type of moral behavior. Understanding the requisite precursors of specific types of prosocial behaviors is important. For example, altruistic behaviors have been the focus of much scrutiny and debate because they are central to understanding human nature. Similarly, compliant behaviors serve many important social functions, including helping to maintain social order and harmony. Furthermore, such behaviors are the building blocks of cooperative and constructive actions that can improve communities and societies and promote global peace. Atlhough moral emotions were directly associated with both forms of helping, prosocial moral reasoning played a mediating role in such relations. Complying with others' request for help and selflessly helping others thus entails contemplation about whether to engage in such actions. Therefore, debates regarding the primacy of emotions and cognitions serve little function in furthering our understanding of morality and moral development. The differential pattern of relations among moral cognitions, emotions, and behaviors suggests that morality results from a complex interplay of such variables. The need is to focus on the integration and delineation of the links among these complex constructs.

Notes

1. Kohlberg, L. (1969). Stage and sequence: The cognitive-developmental approach to socialization. In D. Goslin (Ed.), *Handbook of socialization theory and research*. Stokie, IL: Rand McNally; Turiel, E. (2006). Thought, emotions, and social interactional processes in moral development. In M. Killen & J. G. Smetana (Eds.), *Handbook of moral development* (pp. 7–35). Mahwah, NJ: Erlbaum.

2. Eisenberg, N. (1986). *Altruistic emotion, cognition and behavior.* Mahwah, NJ: Erlbaum; Hoffman, M. L. (2000). *Empathy and moral development: Implications for caring and justice.* Cambridge: Cambridge University Press.

3. Turiel. (2006); Eisenberg. (1986); Piaget, J. (1932/1965). *The moral judgment of the child* (Trans. M. Gabain). London, England: Kegan Paul.

4. Haidt, J. (2001). The emotional dog and its rational tail: A social intuitionist approach to moral judgment. *Psychological Review, 108,* 814–834.

5. Piaget. (1932/1965).

6. Kohlberg. (1969).

7. Gibbs, J. C. (2003). *Moral development and reality: Beyond the theories of Kohlberg and Hoffman.* Thousand Oaks, CA: Sage.

8. Crick, N. R., & Dodge, K. A. (1996). Social information-processing mechanisms on reactive and proactive aggression. *Personality and Social Psychology Bulletin, 67*(3), 993–1002. Eisenberg; (1986); Bandura, A. (1986). *Social foundations of thought and action: A social cognitive theory.* Upper Saddle River, NJ: Prentice Hall; Carlo, G., & Randall, B. (2001). Are all prosocial behaviors equal? A socioecological developmental conception of prosocial behavior. In F. Columbus (Ed.), *Advances in psychology research* (Vol. 2, pp. 151–170). Huntington, NY: Nova Science.

9. Lapsley, D. K. (1996). *Moral psychology.* Boulder, CO: Westview Press.

10. Hoffman. (2000).

11. Hume, D. (1751/1957). *An inquiry concerning the principles of morals.* Indianapolis, IN: Bobbs-Merrill; Blum, L. A. (1980). *Friendship, altruism, and morality.* London: Routledge & Kegan Paul.

12. Eisenberg. (1986); Feshbach, N. D. (1987). Parental empathy and child adjustment/maladjustment. In N. Eisenberg & J. Strayer (Eds.), *Empathy and*

its development (pp. 271–291). Cambridge: Cambridge University Press; Kochanska, G. (1994). Beyond cognition: Expanding the search for the early roots of internalization and conscience. *Developmental Psychology, 30,* 20–22; Thompson, R. A. (1998). Early sociopersonality development. In W. Damon (Series Ed.) & N. Eisenberg (Vol. Ed.), *Handbook of child psychology: Vol. 3. Social, emotional, and personality development* (pp. 25–104). Hoboken, NJ: Wiley; Carlo, G. (2006). Care-based and altruistically-based morality. In M. Killen & J. G. Smetana (Eds.), *Handbook of moral development* (pp. 551–579). Mahwah, NJ: Erlbaum.

13. Carlo. (2006).

14. Harbaugh, W. T., Mayr, U., & Burghart, D. R. (2007). Neural responses to taxation and voluntary giving reveal motives for charitable donations. *Science, 316,* 1622–1625; Loke, I., Evans, A. D., & Lee, K. (2011). The neural correlates of reasoning about prosocial–helping decisions: An event-related brain potentials study. *Brain Research, 1369,* 140–148; Telzer, E. H., Masten, C. L., Berkman, E. T., Lieberman, M. D., & Fuligni, A. J. (2011). Neural regions associated with self control and mentalizing are recruited during prosocial behaviors towards the family. *NeuroImage, 58*(1), 242–249.

15. Kochanska. (1994); Carlo, G., Mestre, M. V., Samper, P., Tur, A., & Armenta, B. E. (2010). Feelings or cognitions? Moral cognitions and emotions as longitudinal predictors of prosocial and aggressive behaviors. *Personality and Individual Differences, 48,* 872–877; Eisenberg, N., Fabes, R. A., Carlo, G., Speer, A. L., Switzer, G., Karbon, M., & Troyer, D. (1993). The relations of empathy-related emotions and maternal practices to children's comforting behavior. *Journal of Experimental Child Psychology, 55,* 131–150; Knight, G. P., Johnson, L. G., Carlo, G., & Eisenberg, N. (1994). A multiplicative model of the dispositional antecedents of a prosocial behavior: Predicting more of the people more of the time. *Journal of Personality and Social Psychology, 66,* 178–183; Eisenberg, N., Guthrie, I. K., Murphy, B. C., Shepard, S. A., Cumberland, A., & Carlo, G. (1999). Consistency and development of prosocial dispositions: A longitudinal study. *Child Development, 70,* 1360–1372.

16. Caro et al.(2010).

17. Eisenberg. (1986); Carlo & Randall. (2001); Blasi, A. (2004). Moral functioning: Moral understanding and personality. In D. K. Lapsley, D. Narvaez, D. K. Lapsley, & D. Narvaez (Eds.), *Moral development, self, and identity* (pp. 335–347). Mahwah, NJ: Erlbaum; Hardy, S. A., & Carlo, G. (2005). Identity as a source of moral motivation. *Human Development, 48,* 232–256.

18. Tangney, J. P., & Dearing, S. (2002). *Shame and guilt.* New York, NY: Guilford Press.

19. Tangney & Dearing. (2002).

20. Hoffman. (2000); Eisenberg, N., Shea, C. L., Carlo, G. & Knight, G. P. (1991). Empathy-related responding and cognition: A "chicken and the egg" dilemma. In W. M. Kurtines & J. L. Gewirtz (Eds.), *Handbook of moral behavior and development. Vol. 2: Research* (pp. 63–88). Mahwah, NJ: Erlbaum.

21. Lapsley, D. K., & Narvaez, D. (2004). A social-cognitive approach to the moral personality. In D. K. Lapsley & D. Narvaez (Eds.), *Moral development, self and identity* (pp. 189–212). Mahwah, NJ: Erlbaum.

22. Tangney & Dearing. (2002); Thompson. (1998); Laible, D., Carlo, G., & Eye, J. (2008). Dimensions of conscience development in mid-adolescence: Links with temperament and parenting. *Journal of Youth and Adolescence, 37*, 875–887.

23. Tangney & Dearing. (2002).

24. Tangney & Dearing. (2002); Fung, H., & Chun, E.C-H. (2001). Across time and beyond skin: Self and transgression in the everyday socialization of shame among Taiwanese preschool children. *Social Development, 10*, 420–437.

25. Hoffman. (2000); Batson, C. D. (1998). Altruism and prosocial behavior. In D. T. Gilbert, S. T. Fiske, & G. Lindzey (Eds.), *The handbook of social psychology* (4th ed., Vol. 2, pp. 282–316). New York, NY: McGraw-Hill; Eisenberg, N., Fabes, R. A., & Spinrad, T. L. (2006). Prosocial development. In W. Damon & R. M. Lerner (Series Eds.) & N. Eisenberg (Vol. Ed.), *Handbook of child psychology, Vol. 3. Social, emotional, and personality development* (6th ed., pp. 646–718). Hoboken, NJ: Wiley.

26. Eisenberg et al. (1991).

27. Carlo (2006); Eisenberg et al. (2006); Carlo, G., Knight, G. P., McGinley, M., Goodvin, R., & Roesch, S. C. (2010). Understanding the developmental relations between perspective taking and prosocial behaviors: A meta-analytic review. In J. Carpendale, G. Iarocci, U. Muller, B. Sokol, & A. Young (Eds.), *Self- and social-regulation: Exploring the relations between social interaction, social cognition, and the development of executive functions* (pp. 234–269). New York, NY: Oxford University Press.

28. Hoffman. (2000); Davis, M. H. (1983). Measuring individual differences in empathy: Evidence for a multidimensional approach. *Journal of Personality and Social Psychology, 44*, 113–126.

29. Kohlberg. (1969).

30. Eisenberg. (1986); Eisenberg et al. (1991).

31. Eisenberg. (1986).

32. Eisenberg et al. (1991); Carlo. (2006).

33. Carlo & Randall. (2001).

34. Carlo, G., & Randall, B. A. (2002). The development of a measure of prosocial behaviors for late adolescents. *Journal of Youth and Adolescence, 31*, 31–44; Carlo, G., Knight, G. P., McGinley, M., Zamboanga, B. L., & Jarvis, L. (2010). The multidimensionality of prosocial behaviors: Evidence of measurement invariance in early Mexican American and European American adolescents. *Journal of Research on Adolescence, 20*, 334–358; Carlo, G., Hausmann, A., Christiansen, S., & Randall, B. A. (2003). Sociocognitive and behavioral correlates of a measure of prosocial tendencies for adolescents. *Journal of Early Adolescence, 23*, 107–134.

35. Carlo et al. (2003).

36. Carlo et al. (2003, 2010).

37. Carlo, G., Eisenberg, N., & Knight, G. P. (1992). An objective measure of adolescents' prosocial moral reasoning. *Journal of Research on Adolescence, 2*, 331–349.

38. Carlo et al. (1992).

39. Davis. (1983).
40. Tangney & Dearing. (2002).
41. Muthén, L. K., & Muthén, B. O. (1998–2010). *Mplus user's guide* (6th ed.). Los Angeles, CA: Muthén & Muthén.
42. Hu, L., & Bentler, P. M. (1999). Cutoff criteria for fit indexes in covariance structure analysis: Conventional criteria versus new alternatives. *Structural Equation Modeling, 6*, 1–55.
43. Davis. (1983).
44. Carlo et al. (1992).
45. Carlo et al. (2010).
46. Eisenberg et al. (1991).
47. Hardy & Carlo. (2005).

GUSTAVO CARLO *is the Millsap Distinguished Professor of Diversity and Multicultural Studies in Human Development and Family Studies at the University of Missouri.*

MEREDITH MCGINLEY *is an assistant professor in counseling psychology at Chatham University.*

ALEXANDRA DAVIS *is a doctoral student in human development and family studies at the University of Missouri.*

CARA STREIT *is a doctoral student in human development and family studies at the University of Missouri.*

Low-income adolescents' negative views of institutional fairness in this study were related to their aggression-related cognitions and behaviors.

6

Adolescents' perceptions of institutional fairness: Relations with moral reasoning, emotions, and behavior

William F. Arsenio, Susanna Preziosi,
Erica Silberstein, Benjamin Hamburger

IN OUR PREVIOUS RESEARCH on the emotional nature of aggression, we asked a sixteen-year-old boy who was rated high in aggression to imagine how he would feel after he knocked someone to the ground to get the last ticket for a special music concert. He replied: "Yeah, I'd be pretty happy I knocked him down. Now I could get the last ticket for the concert, and it was probably going to be a great show. ... The other kid—the kid I knocked down? Yeah, he'd be mad because what I did to him wasn't right."

Most developmental psychologists would explain this pattern of aggression by focusing on early failures in empathic abilities and other forms of moral disengagement.[1] For example, children and adolescents with a related problem (i.e., callous unemotional traits) "show an aberrant affective and interpersonal style that is the hallmark of psychopathy," including a lack of guilt and remorse.[2]

NEW DIRECTIONS FOR YOUTH DEVELOPMENT, NO. 136, WINTER 2012 © WILEY PERIODICALS, INC.
Published online in Wiley Online Library (wileyonlinelibrary.com) • DOI: 10.1002/yd.20041

A complementary view explains these empathic and moral deficits as a product of deficits in the family and neighborhood social resources that usually constrain children's potential aggressive tendencies.[3]

Recently, however, some researchers have adopted the somewhat different view that aggression can at times "be viewed as an adaptive strategy that seeks to order dangerous and unpredictable environments."[4] The focus is not on minimizing the harm and dysfunction associated with aggression, but on understanding whether certain forms of aggression may help adolescents negotiate aspects of their socially toxic environments. These views informed our focus in this article on how low-income, urban adolescents understand the fairness of their larger environments—their economic conditions and legal systems, for example—and how that understanding relates to their interpersonal moral reasoning and self-rated aggressive tendencies. The basic hypothesis is that some adolescents clearly are aware of the unfair nature of their social circumstances and that this awareness may be reflected in their interpersonal moral reasoning, related emotion judgments, and behavior.[5]

Theoretical background

There is extensive evidence that children's understanding of morally relevant transgressions, including aggression, is related to actual moral and aggressive behavior.[6] For example, in their review of child conduct problems, Dodge and Pettit summarize dozens of studies indicating that various peer, familial, and other influences affect children's social reasoning, which in turn affects their behavior. The authors' model of these connections reflects three related propositions: (1) life experiences can lead a child to develop (partially) idiosyncratic social knowledge about his or her world, which is then represented in memory; (2) the child uses that knowledge during social interactions to guide related behaviors; and 3) "the child's pattern of social information processing leads directly to specific social (or antisocial) behaviors and mediates the effects of early life experiences on later chronic conduct problems."[7]

These propositions raise several important pragmatic and moral questions. One key question is whether the idiosyncratic or atypical social cognitions of aggressive and antisocial children are really faulty or inaccurate, and if so by what standard. Alternatively, it could be argued that some of these atypical social cognitions are coherent interpretations of the atypical social realities that many aggressive children experience—for example, socioeconomic deprivation, harsh and erratic parenting, and problematic peer relationships. "Put simply, if a child's daily environment lacks aspects of emotional and moral reciprocity, and tangible elements of fairness, then what kinds of morally-relevant social cognitions should that child be expected to form?"[8] A second question is whether children who have formed these atypical moral cognitions also sometimes attempt to make sense of what has contributed to their atypical social cognitions; they might ask, for example, "Life isn't fair, so why should I be?" Before returning to these questions, we need to offer a brief description of reactive and proactive forms of aggression.

Reactive aggression is often described as a type of frustration response "associated with a lack of control, whereas ... [proactive aggression] appears to be less emotional and more driven by the expectation of award."[9] In general, reactive aggression is predicted by social cognitive deficits—for example, misperceiving ambiguous "provocations," such as being bumped into, as intentional. Proactive aggression, by contrast, is associated with so-called biases, including a strong focus on personal desires rather than concerns with friendships and peer regard and a belief that aggression is an effective means for achieving desired ends. Collectively, the evidence is extensive that the antecedents, correlates, and consequences of reactive and proactive aggression are quite distinct.[10]

Arsenio and Lemerise have argued that this distinction between reactive and proactive also has an important moral dimension that has largely been ignored.[11] In brief, reactive aggressors have the same basic concern with moral fairness and legitimacy as nonaggressive children: both reactive and nonaggressive children believe that it is morally unacceptable ("not fair/right") to intentionally harm or be harmed by others. Reactive aggressive children, however, are less accurate at reading others' intentions and consequently more likely to see provocations where there are none.

By contrast, proactive aggressive children are as accurate at reading others' intentions as nonaggressive children, understand basic moral principles of fairness and justice, and yet seem willing to break those principles when they conflict with personal desires. Proactive aggressors seem to "know the good" without feeling compelled to follow the good.

Recent empirical evidence

Arsenio, Adams, and Gold recently examined these claims in a study of one hundred (sixty-nine of them male) mostly African American and Latino adolescents from a high-risk urban environment.[12] Adolescents were administered a multipart interview that assessed their verbal abilities, moral emotion attributions and reasoning, and multiple aspects of reactive and proactive aggression-related reasoning. In addition, classroom teachers rated these adolescents' aggressive behaviors.

Strikingly different patterns of findings emerged for reactive and proactive aggression. As expected, higher levels of reactive aggression were associated with greater hostile attributional biases (that is, misreading ambiguous but potentially provocative situations) and lower verbal ability, and both of these connections were related to adolescents' attention problems. Reactive aggression, however, was unrelated to adolescents' moral reasoning and emotions. By contrast, adolescents' greater proactive aggressive tendencies were related to (1) higher verbal abilities; (2) greater expectations that moral transgressions, such as stealing a desired jacket, would make one feel happy; and (3) increased explanations of that happiness in terms of desirable gains resulting from victimization.[13]

It is easy to imagine how more reactively aggressive adolescents' weaker verbal skills and difficulties in attending to their social environment could lead to greater frustration, more peer misunderstandings, and ultimately more frequent hostile (that is, hotheaded) aggressive acts. By contrast, proactive aggression was associated with greater expectations of material and emotional rewards resulting from clearly unfair victimization, greater verbal abilities, and no obvious attention problems. Proactive aggression, then, seems to be more than just the product of social cognitive biases: proactive aggressors recognize the harm and unfairness of their actions yet seem relatively unmoved by these concerns.

These findings for proactive aggression seem consistent with explanations described at the start of this article: explanations emphasizing the role of early empathic failures and subsequent moral disengagement. Yet recent research by Fite and colleagues indicates that broader community factors also play a key role in the emergence of proactive aggression. For example, one of their studies found that high levels of neighborhood disadvantage (based on census information) uniquely predicted higher proactive but not reactive aggression.[14] And their separate study on caregivers' perceptions of lower neighborhood safety provided "further evidence for the influence of neighborhood characteristics on proactive, but not reactive aggression."[15]

But why do neighborhood characteristics preferentially influence proactive aggression? One obvious influence is the availability of problematic peer and adult role models in many high-risk neighborhoods. Arsenio and Gold, however, have proposed an additional source of neighborhood influence that has been mostly unexamined:

Developmentally at-risk children must be struck by the same socially toxic nature of their neighborhoods that have been so well documented and described by psychological researchers and other social scientists. And for those children and adolescents unfortunate enough to experience social toxicity … their concepts of fair and just behaviors, not surprisingly are likely to be compromised.[16]

To summarize, there is overwhelming evidence that children and adolescents attempt to understand multiple aspects of their social environments (for example, involving peers and parents), and these social cognitions have important influences on aggression and other morally relevant behaviors. Overall we know a lot about how peers, families, and, to a lesser extent, neighborhoods influence children's morally relevant social reasoning and behavior. To date, however, we know very little about how children and adolescents actively understand, rather than just being influenced by the broader social contexts that shape their lives: neighborhoods, schools, and other institutions. Adolescents' social reasoning is not just a passive product of broad social forces. Instead, adolescents are also clearly active agents who attempt to understand their social worlds, their places in that world, and how they came to occupy those places.

The study

Guided by these ideas, we initiated this research to address several questions:

1. Are adolescents' understanding of interpersonal, peer-focused aggression and morality (the kinds of research typically conducted) related to how they view the fairness and legitimacy of broader social institutions?
2. Are these two types of social reasoning (interpersonal and institutional fairness) related to adolescents' aggressive behaviors?
3. As an important part of this project, what roles do adolescents' moral emotion attributions—how they expect to feel in moral contexts—play in these patterns?

In designing this research, we found numerous techniques for assessing aggression and moral reasoning but far fewer standard methods for assessing adolescents' broad conceptions of institutional fairness. Fortunately, social psychologists have recently become interested in how adults' social reasoning and behavior are affected by a host of political and economic forces.[17] From this larger social psychology literature, we selected three types of measures that we could adapt for use with adolescents, have clear moral relevance (that is, they pose issues of fairness and legitimacy), and have pragmatic importance for the lives of at-risk adolescents.

Before getting into study specifics, we need to provide some background on the institutional measures we selected and what we mean by "institutional fairness." Two of the approaches, involving system justification theory and procedural justice, have been studied extensively in adults, whereas research on the third, perceptions of wealth distribution, is somewhat newer. Starting with system justification, this theory addresses when and why people provide cognitive and ideological support for existing social arrangements, even when that support conflicts with personal and group interests.[18] For example, experimentally manipulating adults' positive stereotypes about the poor in one study (for example, "they're poor but happy") led those adult participants to rate the existing social order more positively on an eight-item scale (for example, "in general, you find society to be fair").[19] More generally, the system justification (or Social Fairness) scale has emerged as a useful tool for assessing judgments about the fairness and legitimacy of the existing social order.

In contrast, procedural justice involves individuals' judgments about the fairness of how they are treated in a various settings—educational, political, organizational, and legal, for example. Numerous studies have shown that perceptions of procedural justice, such as being treated with respect and given a voice in procedures of decision making, are related to viewing authorities as more legitimate, as well as with increased levels of institutional compliance.[20] One of the few studies to include adolescents found that increased levels of legal cynicism (for example, "the law represents the values of people in power, rather than the values of people like you") subsequently predicted higher rates of recidivism in felony juvenile offenders.[21]

The final measure of institutional fairness focuses on the distribution of wealth in the United States and potential economic inequality. Recently two behavioral economists assessed the economic judgments of a nationally representative sample of U.S. adults.[22] After reading a short, standard economic definition of *wealth*, participants engaged in a series of economic judgment tasks. In one task, they estimated the percentage of total U.S. wealth that is actually possessed by each of five equal-sized population quintiles (from the richest 20 percent to the poorest 20 percent), followed by judgments regarding the desired ideal distribution of wealth for each quintile. The overall results were quite surprising. These adult participants radically underestimated actual wealth inequality and preferred fairly egalitarian wealth distributions in their ideal distributions (see Figure 6.1). Moreover,

Figure 6.1. A comparison of U.S. wealth distribution against adults' and adolescents' judgments of estimated and ideal distributions of wealth

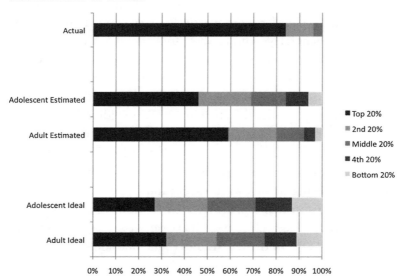

M. I. Norton, & D. Ariely, Building a better America—One wealth quintile at a time. Perspectives on Psychological Science, 6(1). Copyright © 2011 SAGE Publications. Reprinted by Permission of SAGE Publications.

Note: For the actual distribution, shares for the fourth 20 percent value (0.2 percent) and bottom 20 percent value (0.1 percent) are not visible because of their small percentage share of total wealth.

participants' actual and ideal judgments varied much less than expected as a function of their political affiliation, gender, and actual reported income. Adolescents in our study also made judgments about both actual and ideal wealth distributions, and a measure of the discrepancy between these two judgments (labeled "Wealth Disparity") was seen as reflecting the perceived fairness of U.S. wealth distribution.

Study details

To date, we have individually interviewed thirty adolescents (twenty-five male and five female) out of an eventual total of ninety. All thirty adolescents were African American or Latina/o, or both, and came from low-income communities in New York City. Their mean family income was the bottom 25 percent nationally by zip code.

Adolescents were presented with several measures of interpersonal morality and aggression during their interview, in addition to the three measures of institutional fairness and a brief self-rating of reactive and proactive aggressive tendencies.[23] The order of the interpersonal and institutional measures was alternated across participants, but the self-rating for aggression always came last.

Moral reasoning task. Adolescents' moral reasoning and emotion attributions were examined by presenting them with hypothetical stories in which the adolescents deliberately victimized a peer to obtain a clear gain, for example, pushing a peer to the ground to obtain the last ticket for a music concert. Following each story, adolescents judged how they would feel and why.

Social Fairness Scale. This eight-item questionnaire assessed adolescents' "perceptions of the fairness, legitimacy and justifiability of the prevailing social order."[24] Using a five-point scale, participants responded to statements such as, "Everyone has a fair shot at wealth and happiness," and, "Most social policies serve the greater good." Higher scores reflected greater agreement that U.S. society is fair and supports the positive development of its population. In addition, adolescents judged how they felt about current levels of social fairness on a five-point scale.

Legal Cynicism Scale. This four-item measure assessed partici-pants' negative or cynical views regarding the nature of the legal system (for example, "People in power use the law to try to control people like you"), with higher scores indicating more negative views of the legal system.

Wealth ratings. Adolescents were given a brief pretraining ses-sion that included a definition and illustration of wealth and picto-rial aids to illustrate the concept of five equal-sized U.S. population groups, extending from the richest 20 percent to the poorest 20 percent. They then used pie charts to indicate their estimates of how much of total U.S. wealth each of the five groups possessed, followed by judgments of how much, ideally, each income group should possess.

Self-rated aggression. Adolescents used a five-point scale to rate their own reactive (three items) and proactive (three items) aggressive tendencies. One of the reactive self-versions was, "When I get teased or threatened, I get angry easily and strike back," and a proactive self-version was, "I threaten or bully others to get what I want." The selected scale has been validated in numerous studies of children's and adolescents' aggressive tendencies.[25]

Results

We begin with a look at what adolescents as a group thought about larger social institutions. Turning first to the Social Fairness mea-sure, less than a third of adolescents agreed (strongly or somewhat) with the statement, "In general you find society to be fair," and only 40 percent agreed that "everyone has a fair shot at wealth and happiness." In addition, 80 percent of adolescents agreed with the statement that "American society needs to be radically restruc-tured," and 60 percent agreed that "society is getting worse every year." These relatively negative views of society were also mirrored in the measure of adolescents' legal cynicism. Nearly half of the adolescents agreed with the statement, "The law represents the values of the people in power, rather than the values of people like you," and 70 percent agreed with the statement, "People in power use the law to try to control people like you."

By contrast, adolescent's perceptions of wealth distribution provided a somewhat different picture of how they viewed economic fairness. Figure 6.1 shows how adolescents' perceptions of actual and ideal wealth distributions compare with Norton and Ariely's findings from a nationally representative study of adults' perceptions. First, in terms of actual wealth distribution, low-income adolescents, like adults around the United States, radically underestimated the amount of wealth owned by the richest 20 percent. On average, adolescents judged that the richest U.S. quintile owns about 43 percent of all U.S. wealth, whereas adults' estimates averaged around 59 percent. In fact, only one adolescent's judgment approached the true 84 percent of wealth owned by the richest U.S. population quintile. In addition, compared to adults, adolescents overestimated the amount of wealth owned by the poorest 40 percent of the population (16 percent versus 8 percent for adolescents and adults, respectively, compared with an actual total of 0.3 percent). Adolescents and adults, however, were quite similar in at their judgments for ideal wealth distribution.

The findings for our adolescent group are quite consistent with one of Norton and Ariely's major conclusions:

Given the consensus among disparate groups on the gap between an ideal distribution of wealth and the actual level of wealth inequality, why are more Americans, especially those with low income, not advocating for greater redistribution of wealth? First, our results demonstrate that Americans appear to drastically underestimate the current level of wealth inequality, suggesting they may simply be unaware of the gap.[26]

As a group, the low-income adolescents in this study had quite negative views of the fairness and opportunities offered by U.S. society as a whole, as well as negative views regarding the legal system. Yet like most U.S. adults, these adolescents fundamentally underestimated the wealth distribution in the United States, while also sharing the general view that a much more egalitarian wealth distribution would be preferable.

In the following sections, we briefly examine some of the connections among adolescents' self-rated aggression, conceptions of institutional fairness, and moral emotion attributions and reasoning.

Aggressive tendencies and institutional fairness. Adolescents' self-rated aggressive tendencies had several interesting connections with reasoning about institutional and interpersonal fairness. As might be expected, adolescents with higher proactive but not reactive aggressive tendencies (accurately) judged that the wealthiest 20 percent of American possessed greater amounts of total U.S. wealth. Another finding involved wealth disparity—the difference between each individual's estimate for the wealth owned by the richest 20 percent minus the ideal wealth that the richest 20 percent should own. Adolescents with higher proactive (but not reactive) aggressive tendencies also perceived greater U.S. wealth disparities. In other words, more proactively aggressive adolescents perceived greater gaps between "what exists" and what "should exist" when it comes to the wealth controlled by the richest 20 percent of Americans.

Findings for the other measures of institutional fairness were less clear. There were no significant connections between adolescents' reactive or proactive aggressive tendencies and their judgments on the Social Fairness scale. Furthermore, adolescents' scores on legal cynicism were related to reactive and proactive aggressive tendencies in unexpected ways. Specifically, their higher proactive aggressive tendencies were related to lower levels of legal cynicism, whereas reactive aggressive tendencies were related to higher levels of legal cynicism.

Aggressive tendencies and interpersonal emotions and fairness. Adolescents' aggressive tendencies had several revealing connections with the emotions they expected to feel after victimizing others (the moral reasoning task). Adolescents with higher proactive aggressive tendencies expected to feel more "okay" after victimizing others, whereas adolescents with higher reactive aggressive tendencies expected to feel more fearful and less sad after victimizing others. Their explanations for these emotions, however, were not related to their aggressive tendencies.

Although these results support the importance of adolescents' moral emotion attributions, the specific findings also differ from some previous research.[27] For example, Arsenio and colleagues found that adolescents with higher proactive aggressive tendencies expected to feel happier following acts of victimization.[28] By contrast, our findings suggest that expecting to feel neutral or okay following victimizing acts is also problematic. It is noteworthy, however, that in both studies, adolescents' selection of nonnegative emotions following victimizing acts was related to higher levels of proactive aggression.

Interpersonal and institutional fairness. A number of connections were found between adolescents' conceptions of institutional and interpersonal fairness. First, adolescents with higher levels of legal cynicism expected to feel less emotionally negative (sad, angry, or scared) following their victimization of others. In addition, adolescents who judged that U.S. society as a whole is less fair or felt negatively about that lack of fairness expected to feel less afraid after victimizing others. Adolescents' rationales for their interpersonal emotions, however, had no connections with their conceptions of institutional fairness.

Conclusion

One major study conclusion is that these adolescents collectively have a fairly negative view of the fairness and opportunities offered by U.S. society. Fewer than half of the adolescents believed that society in general is fair or that "everyone has a fair shot at wealth and happiness," and a great majority agreed that America needs to be radically restructured and that the law largely represents the values of the people in power. As one fourteen-year-old adolescent put it, "The people with the most money have the most resources, the best SAT [preparation] programs, best schools, and better chance of succeeding. ... Your parents having money shouldn't affect it, but it does." Yet these adolescents, like the adults in the Norton and Ariely study, also radically underestimated the actual concentration of wealth in the United States.[29] We draw two major conclusions from these findings. First, low-income adolescents have a rich and revealing understanding of institutional fairness that deserves to be studied on its own terms. And, second, as a group, Americans have a very poor understanding of how U.S. wealth is actually distributed, even though they strongly agree that it should be divided more equally.

Another major conclusion is that adolescents also differed from one another in how they viewed institutional fairness; as expected, some of these differences related to their morally relevant reasoning and behavior. One key finding is that more proactively (but not reactively) aggressive adolescents correctly judged that the wealthiest 20 percent of Americans own a larger portion of total U.S. wealth. In addition, more proactively aggressive adolescents expected to feel more "okay" following their hypothetical victimization of others. Taken together, these findings provide initial support for our central claim that some adolescents are aware of the unfair nature of their larger circumstances and that this awareness may be reflected in their moral reasoning, anticipated emotions, and behavior.

Finally, a few closing caveats are in order. Our findings are based on responses from thirty adolescents out of an eventual total of ninety participants: consequently, some of the specific findings reported here may change slightly as we interview more adolescents. We also acknowledge a limited number of connections between adolescents' perceptions of institutional fairness and their interpersonal reasoning and behavior. Additional research is needed to address these concerns and provide a better sense of how low-income adolescents' perceptions of institutional fairness compare with the perceptions of their more economically advantaged peers.

Notes

1. Baron-Cohen, S. (2011). *The science of evil: On empathy and the origins of cruelty.* New York, NY: Basic Books; Bandura, A., Barbaranelli, C., Caprara, G., & Pastorelli, C. (1996). Mechanisms of moral disengagement in the exercise of moral agency. *Journal of Personality and Social Psychology, 71,* 364–374.

2. Marsee, M., & Frick, P. (2010). Callous-unemotional traits and aggression in youth. In W. Arsenio & E. Lemerise (Eds.), *Emotions, aggression, and morality in children: Bridging development and psychopathology* (pp. 137–156). Washington, DC; American Psychological Association. P. 138.

3. Hyde, L., Shaw, D., & Moilanen, K. (2010). Developmental precursors of moral disengagement and the role of moral disengagement in the development of antisocial behavior. *Journal of Abnormal Child Psychology, 38*(2), 197–209.

4. Wilkinson, D., & Carr, P. (2008). Violent youths' responses to high levels of exposure to community violence: What violent events reveal about youth violence. *Journal of Community Psychology, 36*(8), 1026–1051. P. 1026.

5. Arsenio, W., & Gold, J. (2006). The effects of social injustice and inequality on children's moral judgments and behavior: Towards a theoretical model. *Cognitive Development, 21,* 388–400.

6. Turiel, E. (2006). The development of morality. In W. Damon & R. Lerner (Series Eds.) & N. Eisenberg (Vol. Ed.), *Handbook of child psychology. Vol. 3: Social, emotional, and personality development* (6th ed., pp. 789–780). Hoboken, NJ: Wiley.

7. Dodge, K., & Pettit, G. (2003). A biopsychosocial model of the development of chronic conduct disorders in adolescence. *Developmental Psychology, 39,* 349–371.

8. Arsenio & Gold. (2006). P. 390.

9. Dodge, K., Lochman, J., Harnish, J., Bates, J., & Pettit, G. (1997). Reactive and proactive aggression in school children and psychiatrically impaired chronically assaultive youth. *Journal of Abnormal Psychology, 106,* 37–51. P. 38.

10. Hubbard, J., McAuliffe, M., Morrow, M., & Romano, L. (2010). Reactive and proactive aggression in childhood and adolescence: Precursors, outcomes, processes, experiences, and measurement. *Journal of Personality, 78*(1), 95–118.

11. Arsenio, W., & Lemerise, E. (2001). Varieties of childhood bullying: Values, emotion processes, and social competence. *Social Development, 10,* 59–73.

12. Arsenio, W., Adams, E., & Gold, J. (2009). Social information processing, moral reasoning, and emotion attributions: Relations with adolescents' reactive and proactive aggression. *Child Development, 80*(6), 1739–1755.

13. For the "happy-victimizer" literature, see Arsenio, W. F., Gold, J., & Adams, E. (2006). Children's conceptions and displays of moral emotions. In M. Killen & J. Smetana (Eds.), *Handbook of moral development* (pp. 581–608). Mahwah, NJ: Erlbaum.

14. Fite, P., Wynn, P., Lochman, J., & Wells, K. (2009). The effect of neighborhood disadvantage on proactive and reactive aggression. *Journal of Community Psychology, 37*(4), 542–546.

15. Fite, P., Vitulano, M., Wynn, P., Wimsatt, A., Gaertner, A., & Rathert, J. (2010). Influence of perceived neighborhood safety on proactive and reactive aggression. *Journal of Community Psychology, 38*(6), 757–768. P. 766.

16. Arsenio & Gold. (2006). P. 397.

17. Jost, J., Banaji, M., & Nosek, B. (2004). A decade of system justification theory: Accumulated evidence of conscious and unconscious bolstering of the status quo. *Political Psychology, 25*(6), 881–917.

18. Jost et al. (2004).

19. Kay, A., & Jost, J. (2003). Complementary justice: The effects of "poor but happy" and "poor but honest" stereotype exemplars on system justification and implicit activation of the justice motive. *Journal of Personality and Social Psychology, 85*(5), 823–837.

20. Tyler, T. (2006). Psychological perspectives on legitimacy and legitimation. *Annual Review of Psychology, 57*, 375–400.

21. Fagan, J., & Piquero, A. (2007). Rational choice and developmental influences on recidivism among adolescent felony offenders. *Journal of Empirical Legal Studies, 4*(4), 715–748.

22. Norton, M., & Ariely, D. (2011). Building a better American—one wealth quintile at a time. *Perspectives on Psychological Science, 6*(1), 9–12.

23. The measures of interpersonal morality and aggression during their interview are from Arsenio et al. (2009).

24. Kay & Jost. (2003). P. 828.

25. Hubbard et al. (2010).

26. Norton & Ariely. (2011). P. 12.

27. Malti, T., & Ongley, S. (in press). The development of moral emotions and reasoning. In M. Killen & J. Smetana (Eds.), *Handbook of moral development*. New York, NY: Taylor & Francis.

28. Arsenio et al. (2009).

29. Norton & Ariely. (2011).

WILLIAM F. ARSENIO *is a professor of psychology at the Ferkauf Graduate School of Psychology, Yeshiva University.*

SUSANNA PREZIOSI *is a clinical graduate student at the Ferkauf Graduate School of Psychology, Yeshiva University.*

ERICA SILBERSTEIN *is a clinical graduate student at the Ferkauf Graduate School of Psychology, Yeshiva University.*

BENJAMIN HAMBURGER *is a clinical graduate student at the Ferkauf Graduate School of Psychology, Yeshiva University.*

Mindfulness provides a promising tool to reduce distress and promote resilience by helping adolescents navigate their psychological and environmental challenges.

7

Mindfulness for adolescents: A promising approach to supporting emotion regulation and preventing risky behavior

Patricia C. Broderick, Patricia A. Jennings

DEMANDS TO MEET the increasing pace of change are creating unprecedented challenges for educators and parents to equip students with the knowledge and skills they need to succeed in school and in life. There is growing recognition that social and emotional skills and dispositions are essential for flexible decision making, stress hardiness, lifelong learning, and innovation required to maintain prosperity and civility in a rapidly changing world.[1]

Competence in social and emotional skills provides the foundation for learning to manage one's life effectively. It encompasses knowing how to channel attention and sustain motivation, working cooperatively with others, coping with frustration, responding to challenges with appropriate behavior, and avoiding risky behaviors. Decades of research have reliably demonstrated that well-designed and well-implemented classroom-based prevention programs can reduce conduct problems while building skills for mental health,

NEW DIRECTIONS FOR YOUTH DEVELOPMENT, NO. 136, WINTER 2012 © WILEY PERIODICALS, INC.
Published online in Wiley Online Library (wileyonlinelibrary.com) • DOI: 10.1002/yd.20042

interpersonal relationships, and academic achievement. Although there are many evidenced-based programs for younger children, few well-established evidence-based programs exist for adolescents, a significant educational gap.[2] Adolescence is a time of major cognitive advances and gains in physical strength and vitality, but this period of development is also distinguished by the onset of many physical, behavioral, and mental health problems that are preventable and may persist into adulthood, interfering with educational achievement and work productivity in long-lasting ways.

Evidence from large-scale epidemiological studies suggests the global importance of adolescent health.[3] According to the U.S. Surgeon General's report, one out of five children and adolescents in the United States suffers from significant social, emotional, and behavioral problems that place them at risk for school failure.[4] A 1993 report by the American Academy of Pediatrics on threats to adolescent well-being was updated in 2001 to include school problems (including learning disabilities and attention difficulties), mood and anxiety disorders, adolescent suicide and homicide, firearms in the home, school violence, drug and alcohol abuse, HIV/AIDS, and the effects of media on violence, obesity, and sexual activity. Most of these social and emotional risks, referred to as "new morbidities," are amplified by emotional and behavioral dysregulation.[5]

Contemporary adolescents face a host of developmental challenges that can threaten their physical and emotional well-being, including disengagement from school, alienation from parents, body image self-consciousness, susceptibility to peer influence, pressure to engage in sexual activity and romantic relationships, participation in antisocial or risky behaviors, and heavy exposure to media that may mold behavioral expectations at odds with the values of their families and communities.[6] Adolescents report high levels of school-related stress associated with homework, tests, expectations for achievement, and interactions with teachers.[7] The time pressures that challenge so many adults also affect the younger generation.[8] To meet these challenges successfully requires a high level of social and emotional competence.

Neurobiological changes of adolescence

In addition to these challenges, evidence is growing that adolescence is a sensitive period for stress as a result of puberty-related changes in hormones and dramatic plasticity in the structure and function of the brain.[9] Conditions for optimal brain development during adolescence are still uncertain, but new research on emotion and behavior regulation, emotional information processing, and stress reactivity has demonstrated that adolescence is a period of particular vulnerability to the social and emotional environment.

Adolescents process emotional information differently from the way prepubertal children and adults do. For example, recent research suggests increased limbic reactivity (sensitivity to threat), exaggerated startle reflex (a measure of fear processing), and stronger interference effects from emotional stimuli on task completion during adolescence.[10] These findings lend support to the proposition that the adolescent brain is particularly reactive to emotional information.[11]

Brain development that occurs during adolescence primarily involves changes in the frontal and parietal cortices, the site of executive functions—higher-order cognitive and socioemotional processes. A peak in gray matter volume at puberty is followed by a gradual decline as the cortex is fine-tuned through synaptic pruning in areas that play a role in judgment, impulse control, planning, and emotion regulation.[12] As in childhood, experience-dependent learning also plays a part in the sculpting of the brain at adolescence.

Effects of stress in adolescence

These rapid neurobiological changes may predispose adolescents to be uniquely sensitive to the effects of stress.[13] While the human stress response is adaptive in short bursts and helps mobilize energy reserves for goal-directed purposes, prolonged stress or dysregulated responsiveness can have a negative effect on health, learning, and productivity.[14] Executive functions such as the ability to direct attention and solve problems efficiently show clear stress-induced disruptions, particularly when there is a perceived lack of control over stressors.[15] Whereas mild stress can enhance memory, chronic or excessive stress can result in damage to parts of the brain critical for new learning and memory consolidation.[16]

Given the potentially harmful lifetime consequences of a chronically overactivated stress system, it is critically important to consider the effects of stress on adolescents' developing brains. Hormones play a role in laying down new neural pathways during adolescence, so overexpression of and increased sensitivity to cortisol, the major stress hormone, during this period of rapid brain reorganization may signal a window of vulnerability for the development of psychopathology.[17]

Normally developing adolescents, compared to younger and older groups, display heightened stress reactivity on cortisol and other autonomic nervous system measures during challenging situations.[18] Perceived stress, mental anticipation of a stressor, and memories about past stressors and peer rejection have particularly strong associations with cardiac and cortisol reactivity among adolescents.[19] Considering this evidence, the "intersection of stress and the developing adolescent brain may represent a 'perfect storm' in the context of dysfunctional emotional development."[20]

The importance of emotion regulation

Emotion regulation involves strategies to manage distress in order to meet the demands of different situations or achieve certain goals, such as those involved in learning, and is increasingly viewed by contemporary researchers as a foundation for well-being, academic achievement, and positive adjustment throughout the life span.[21] Emotion regulation processes include identification and acceptance of emotional experiences, management of distress and modulation of excitement, sustaining motivation, prioritizing among competing goals, and adaptive adjustment of behavioral responses. Difficulties in emotion regulation are a core feature of many adolescent-onset emotional and behavioral problems, including depression, anxiety, conduct problems, deliberate self-injury, disordered eating, and substance use and abuse.[22]

Heightened emotional distress predicts behavior problems and academic failure.[23] Adolescents with low distress tolerance are significantly more likely to engage in harmful risk-taking behavior than those with greater capacity for distress tolerance despite similar risk taking propensity.[24] Roeser and his colleagues suggest that emotional distress disrupts the learning process through several mechanisms, including the reduction of self-regulatory efficacy and academic motivation and the amplification of experiential avoidance.[25]

If adolescence is a stress-sensitive period of development, then emotional distress may be a risk factor for emotional and behavioral problems for all adolescents. Therefore, we need to prioritize effective universal prevention programs that teach emotion regulation (distress tolerance) skills to all adolescents, not just to those at increased risk of problems, as part of comprehensive social and emotional language programming. We propose that a mindfulness-based approach may be uniquely suited to this task.

The contribution of mindfulness for training attention and emotion regulation

Mindfulness is a term used to describe a particular kind of attention that is characterized by intentionality, present moment focus, and nonevaluative observation of experience.[26] It can also refer to the act of paying attention in this way (that is, being mindful). All of these attributes can be developed by the practice of intentionally directing and maintaining attention on targets such as the breath or sensory input as in meditation or mindful awareness practice. During practice, attention is purposefully directed to phenomena as they occur in the present moment. Mindful attention is marked by curiosity and openness to the nature of the experience and the quality of the attention itself. In this context, *nonjudgment* refers to the dual capacity to notice that one's attention can be captured by thoughts and emotions about experience and that this automatic tendency can be countered by intentionally exploring the experience without preconceptions.

Maladaptive behaviors such as aggression and procrastination may become impulsive automatic responses to emotional distress (for example, anger or anxiety) or perceptions of unpleasantness (for example, boredom). Mindfulness is particularly suited to addressing these tendencies to respond in automatic, nonconscious ways to triggers, sometimes referred to as *automatic pilot*. The practice of an attentive and nonreactive attitude toward one's impulses may "increase the gap between impulse and action."[27] Regularly practicing mindfulness may allow elements of conscious and less conscious experience to be perceived from a decentered, decontextualized, and more accepting stance. This approach may disrupt reactivity, strengthen attention, and bring problem solving and behavior under more conscious and reflective regulation.[28]

Research on the effects of mindfulness training with adults has shown numerous benefits, including enhanced awareness of bodily sensation and improved emotion regulation and attention, especially in advanced meditators but also after a brief period of meditation training.[29] Benefits also include increases in positive mood and immune system functioning, reductions in depressive relapse, greater empathy, reductions in substance abuse, and reduced stress.[30]

Although research with adolescents is more limited, some studies have documented improvements in attention skills; social skills for students with learning disabilities; sleep quality; well-being in adolescent boys; and reductions in anxiety, depression, somatic, and externalizing symptoms in clinic-referred adolescents.[31] More research using rigorous experimental designs is needed to assess the effects of mindfulness-based approaches among youth, particularly approaches that can be integrated into ongoing high school curricula as universal prevention.[32] One example of such a program is the Learning to BREATHE classroom-based program.

Learning to BREATHE: A universal prevention program

Learning to BREATHE (L2B) is a developmentally appropriate universal prevention program designed to be integrated into secondary educational settings. The program aims to increase emotion regulation, improve stress management, and promote executive functions in order to promote well-being and support learning. Adapting themes from mindfulness-based stress reduction developed by Kabat-Zinn, the L2B is shorter, more accessible to students, and compatible with school curricula.[33] The program includes instruction in the practice of mindful awareness and provides opportunities for group and individual practice. Since L2B objectives are explicitly linked to standards for health, counseling, and other professional areas, the program may be incorporated into existing curricula.

The core curriculum may be adapted for various configurations of students in six, twelve, or eighteen sessions within a health, school counseling, or other curriculum area. Each lesson includes a short introduction of the topic, several group activities and discussion, and an opportunity for in-class mindfulness practice. *Mindfulness practice*, as used here, refers to the practice of training the mind to pay attention in a particular way: on purpose, in the present moment, and with nonjudgmental openness.[34] Several short practices are taught, including body scan, awareness of thoughts, awareness of feelings, and loving-kindness practices. Loving-kindness practice supports self-compassion and compassion for others.[35] Workbooks and CDs for home mindfulness practice accompany this program.

The six major themes of the L2B curriculum are built around the BREATHE acronym:

B (Body): body awareness.

R (Reflections): understanding and working with thoughts.

E (Emotions): understanding and working with feelings.

A (Attention): integrating awareness of thoughts, feelings, and bodily sensations.

T ("Take it as it is"): reducing harmful self-judgments and increasing acceptance.

H (Healthy habits of mind): cultivating positive emotions and integrating mindfulness into daily life.

E: The overall goal of the program, to cultivate emotional balance and inner empowerment through the practice of mindfulness, an advantage referred to as gaining the "inner edge."

Theory of change, developmental assumptions, and empirical support

The L2B program assumes that the practice of mindful awareness will affect student academic and behavioral outcomes by reducing stress and increasing distress tolerance, strengthening executive functions, promoting emotion and behavioral regulation, and ultimately supporting academic goals.[36] For the purposes of this model, stress is defined as the experience of conscious or nonconscious emotions and patterns of reactivity, such as anxiety, boredom, irritation, and impulsivity, that cause regulatory processes to deteriorate and impede goal-directed behavior. Figure 7.1 illustrates a model in which typical reactions to stress (distress) trigger pathways to emotional regulation or chronic dysregulation.

First, internal or external conditions trigger the perception of distress. Ineffective management of internal distress that dysregulates behavior can disrupt accomplishments in important areas of adolescent functioning. Second, maladaptive response patterns develop, taking the form of avoidance of or overengagement with the distressing situation in an effort to reduce distress. For example, adolescents may seek to numb feelings of social rejection by engaging in risky behavior. Distress is temporarily blunted, and the

Figure 7.1. Conceptual model of L2B

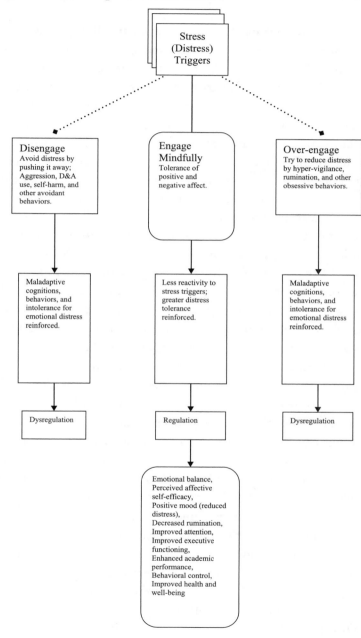

maladaptive behavior is reinforced, strengthening dysfunctional patterns.

Maladaptive behaviors provide transient relief (positive reinforcement) and serve to permit escape from emotional pain (negative reinforcement). Alternatively, adolescents might become preoccupied with their distress in ways that reinforce the associations between automatic thoughts and negative affect—for example, obsessive worry or rumination, which is constant reexamination or reexperiencing of a distressing situation in a misguided effort to resolve problems and regulate emotions. Rumination heightens attention to distress cues, amplifies rather than attenuates distress, and reduces the capacity of working memory to engage in learning effectively.[37]

The practice of mindfulness may restore balance when strong emotions arise by increasing metacognitive awareness of mental processes that contribute to emotion dysregulation. Since emotions are transitory, it is useful to practice noticing emotions on the spot. Mindfulness practice offers the opportunity to develop hardiness in the face of uncomfortable feelings that otherwise might provoke a behavioral response that may be harmful to self and others. Furthermore, mindfulness practice strengthens attention by repeatedly orienting attention to a specific object of focus while consciously letting go of distractions. Mindfulness practice involves intentionally sustaining focused attention, and in this way it strengthens the executive skill of inhibition. Through mindfulness practice, automatic processes may come under more conscious control, fostering reflective decision making and reducing impulsive reactions. The practice of orienting to experience with curiosity, patience, and nonjudgment strengthens tolerance for distress and may reduce the adolescent tendency to overappraise threat, providing a potential protective factor against stressors. Over time, the practice of tolerating experience as it arises without engaging in automatic reactions can strengthen resilience and support affective regulatory self-efficacy and control.

This approach is based on certain assumptions about adolescent development.[38] At a deep psychological level, adolescents are involved with constructing an identity and developing autonomy from adults, a task that can be overwhelming and confusing. Although adolescents have the ability to understand and manage their emotions, education in this area has been neglected in school settings. The discussion and practice included in L2B support adolescents' increased capacity for introspection while maintaining sensitivity to their internal pressure for social conformity and tendency for social comparison.

Learning to BREATHE has been implemented in a variety of settings, including private (residential and nonresidential) and public middle and secondary schools, clinical settings, and after-school programs. Overall, improvements in emotion regulation skills and reductions in psychosomatic symptoms and reported stress were consistently observed. Adolescents who participated in the program were better able to recognize and label feelings, were less anxious and reactive to difficult thoughts and feelings, and showed a greater array of coping abilities.[39] Although results are encouraging, clearly more research is needed.

Conclusion

The adolescent period is marked by changes, particularly brain changes, that are "among the most dramatic and important to occur during the human lifespan."[40] Recent research has affirmed the importance of supporting adolescents through this transition period as they build the physical and mental competencies that will contribute to the course of their adulthood. Mindfulness practice has tremendous power to support healthy development during adolescence and beyond by reducing stress, fostering wellness, and providing tools for emotional balance. Particularly for youth, cultivation of these faculties of mind has direct relevance to burgeoning self-awareness, self-regulation, and the emotional balance that supports fully engaged learning and well-being. It is of great importance that educators and professionals help adolescents find the inner reserves of mindful awareness that are available to them.

Notes

1. Collaborative for Academic, Social, and Emotional Learning. (2008). *Social and emotional learning and student benefits: Implications for the Safe School/Healthy Students core elements.* Washington, DC: National Center for Mental Health Promotion and Youth Violence Prevention, Education Development Center.

2. Greenberg, M. T., Kusche, C. A., Cook, E. T., & Quamma, J. P. (1995). Promoting emotional competence in school-aged children: The effects of the PATHS curriculum. *Development and Psychopathology, 7,* 117–136.

3. Patel, V., Flisher, A. J., Heetrick, S., & McGorry, P. (2007). Mental health of young people: A global public health challenge. *Lancet, 369,* 1302–1313.

4. U.S. Public Health Service. (2000). *Report of the Surgeon General's Conference on Children's Mental Health: A national action agenda.* Washington, DC: Department of Health and Human Services.

5. Dahl, R. E. (2004). Adolescent brain development: A period of vulnerabilities and opportunities. *Annals of the New York Academy of Sciences, 1021,* 1–22.

6. Gutman, L. M., Sameroff, A. J., & Cole, R. (2003). Academic trajectories from first to twelfth grades: Growth curves according to multiple risk and early child factors. *Developmental Psychology, 39,* 777–790; Darling, N., Cumsille, P., & Martinez, M. L. (2008). Individual differences in adolescents' beliefs about the legitimacy of parental authority and their own obligation to obey: A longitudinal investigation. *Child Development, 79,* 1103–1118; Rodriguez-Tome, H., Bariaud, F., Zardi, M. F., & Cohen Delmas, C. (1993). The effects of pubertal changes on body image and relations with peers of the opposite sex in adolescence. *Journal of Adolescence, 16,* 421–438; Sim, T. N., & Koh, S. F. (2003). A domain conceptualization of adolescent susceptibility to peer pressure. *Journal of Research on Adolescence, 13,* 57–80; Collins, W. A. (2003). More than myth: The developmental significance of romantic relationships during adolescence. *Journal of Research on Adolescence, 13,* 1–24; Reyna, V. F., & Farley, F. (2006). Risk and rationality in adolescent decision making: Implications for theory, practice, and public policy. *Psychological Science in the Public Interest, 7,* 1–44; Comstock, G., & Scharrer, E. (2006). Media and popular culture. In W. Damon & R. M. Lerner (Series Eds.), K. A. Renninger, & I. E. Sigel (Vol. Eds.), *Handbook of child psychology: Vol. 4. Child psychology in practice* (6th ed., pp. 817–863). Hoboken, NJ: Wiley.

7. Jacobshagen, N., Rigotti, T., Semmer, N. K., & Mohr, G. (2009). Irritation at school: Reasons to initiate strain management earlier. *International Journal of Stress Management, 16,* 195–214.

8. Melman, S., Little, S. G., & Akin-Little, A. (2007). Adolescent overscheduling: The relationship between levels of participation in scheduled activities and self-reported clinical symptomology. *High School Journal, 90,* 18–30.

9. Romeo, R. D. (2010). Adolescence: A central event in shaping stress reactivity. *Developmental Psychobiology, 52,* 244–253.

10. Silk, J. S., Siegel, G. J., Whalen, D. J., Ostapenko, L. J., Ladoucer, C. D., & Dahl, R. E. (2009). Pubertal changes in emotional information processing:

Pupillary, behavioral, and subjective evidence during emotional work identification. *Development and Psychopathology, 21,* 7–26; Thomas, K. M., Drevets, W. C., Whalen, P. J., Eccard, C. H., Dahl, R. E., & Ryan, N. D. (2001). Amygdala response to facial expressions in children and adults. *Biological Psychiatry, 49,* 309–316. Quevedo, K., Benning, S. D., Gunnar, M. R., & Dahl, R. E. (2009). The onset of puberty: Effects on the psychophysiology of defensive and appetitive motivation. *Development and Psychopathology, 21,* 27–45; Hare, T. A., Tottenham, N., Galvan, A., Voss, H. U., Glover, G. H., & Casey, B. J. (2008). Biological substrates of emotional reactivity and regulation in adolescence during an emotional go-nogo task. *Biological Psychiatry, 63,* 927–934.

11. Blakemore, S. J. (2008). Development of the social brain during adolescence. *Quarterly Journal of Experimental Psychology, 61,* 40–49; Casey, B. J., Jones, R. M., & Hare, T. A. (2008). The adolescent brain. *Annals of the New York Academy of Sciences, 1124,* 111–126.

12. Giedd, J. N., Blumenthal, J., Jeffrie, N. O., Castellanos, F. X., Liu, H., Zijdenbos, A., ... Rapoport, J. L. (1999). Brain development during childhood and adolescence: A longitudinal MRI study. *Nature Neuroscience, 2,* 861–863; Casey, B. J., Giedd, J. N., & Thomas, K. M. (2000). Structural and functional brain development and its relation to cognitive development. *Biological Psychology, 54,* 241–257.

13. Romeo. (2010).

14. McEwen, B. S. (2003). Mood disorders and allostatic load. *Biological Psychiatry, 54,* 200–207.

15. Arnsten, A. F. T., & Shansky, R. M. (2004). Adolescent vulnerable period for stress-induced prefrontal cortical function? Introduction to part IV. *Annals of the New York Academy of Sciences, 1021,* 143–147.

16. Andersen, S. L., & Teicher, M. H. (2008). Stress, sensitive periods and maturational events in adolescent depression. *Trends in Neuroscience, 31,* 183–191.

17. Spear. (2009).

18. Stroud, L., Foster, E., Handwerger, K., Papandonatos, G. D., Granger, D., Kivilighan, K. T., & Niaura, R. (2009). Stress response and the adolescent transition: Performance versus peer rejection stress. *Development and Psychopathology, 21,* 47–68.

19. Sumter, S. R., Bokhorsta, C. L., Miersa, A. C., Van Pelt, J., & Westenberg, P. M. (2010). Age and puberty differences in stress responses during a public speaking task: Do adolescents grow more sensitive to social evaluation? *Psychoneuroendocrinology, 35,* 1510–1516; Sebastian, C., Viding, E., Williams, K. D., & Blakemore, S. J. (2010). Social brain development and the affective consequences of ostracism in adolescence. *Brain and Cognition, 72,* 134–145.

20. Romeo. (2010).

21. Campos, J. J., Frankel, C. B., & Camras, L. (2004). On the nature of emotion regulation. *Child Development, 75,* 377–394; Eisenberg, N., Spinrad, T. L., & Eggum, N. D. (2010). Emotion-related self-regulation and its relationship to children's maladjustment. *Annual Review of Clinical Psychology, 6,* 495–525.

22. Beato-Fernández, L., Rodríguez-Cano, T., Pelayo-Delgado, E., & Calaf, M. (2007). Are there gender-specific pathways from early adolescence psychological distress symptoms toward the development of substance use and abnormal eating behavior? *Child Psychiatry and Human Development*, *37*, 193–203; Cisler, J. M., Olatunji, B. O., Felder, M. T., & Forsyth, J. P. (2010). Emotion regulation and the anxiety disorders. *Journal of Psychopathology and Behavioral Assessment*, *32*, 68–82; Laye-Gindhul, A., & Schonert-Reichl, K. A. (2005). Nonsuicidal self-harm among community adolescents: Understanding the "whats" and "whys" of self-harm. *Journal of Youth and Adolescence*, *34*, 447–457.

23. Needham, B. L., Crosnoe, R., & Muller, C. (2004). Academic failure in secondary school: The inter-related role of health problems and educational context. *Social Problems*, *51*, 569–586.

24. MacPherson, L., Reynolds, E. K., Daughters, S. B., Wang, F., Cassidy, J., Mayes, L. C., & Lejuez, C.W. (2010). Positive and negative reinforcement underlying risk behavior in early adolescents. *Prevention Science*, *11*, 331–342.

25. Roeser, R. W., Vanderwolf, K., & Strobel, K. R. (2001). On the relation between social-emotional and school functioning during early adolescence: Preliminary findings from Dutch and American samples. *Journal of School Psychology*, *39*, 111–139.

26. Kabat-Zinn, J. (1994). *Wherever you go, there you are: Mindfulness meditation in everyday life*. New York, NY: Hyperion.

27. Boyce, B. (2005). Two sciences of the mind. *Shambhala Sun*, *13*, 34–43, 93–96. P. 40.

28. Zelazo, P. D., & Cunningham, W. (2007). Executive function: Mechanisms underlying emotion regulation. In J. Gross (Ed.), *Handbook of emotion regulation* (pp. 135–158). New York, NY: Guilford Press.

29. Lazar, S., Kerr, C., Wasserman, R., Gray, J., Greve, D., Treadway, M., McGarvey, M., ... Fischl, B. (2005). Meditation experience is associated with increased cortical thickness. *NeuroReport*, *16*, 1893–1897; Desbordes, G., Negi, L. T, Pace, T.W.W., Wallace, B. A., Raison, C. L., & Schwartz, E. L. (2012). Effects of mindful-attention and compassion meditation training on amygdala response to emotional stimuli in an ordinary, non-meditative state. *Frontiers in Human Neuroscience*. doi: 10.3389/fnhum.2012.00292; Jha, A. P., Stanley, E. A., Kiyonaga, A., Wong, L., & Gelfand, L. (2010). Examining the protective effects of mindfulness training on working memory and affective experience. *Emotion*, *10*, 54–64; van den Hurk, P.A.M., Giommi, F., Gielen, S. C., Speckens, A. E. M., & Barendregt, H. P. (2010), Greater efficiency in attentional processing related to mindfulness meditation. *Quarterly Journal of Experimental Psychology*, *63*, 1168–1180; Tang, Y., Ma, Y., Fan, Y., Fend, H., Wang, J., Feng, S., ... & Fan, M. (2009). Central and autonomic nervous system interaction is altered by short-term meditation. *Proceedings of the National Academy of Sciences*, *106*, 8865–8870; Zeidan, F., Johnson, S. K., Diamond, B. J., David, Z., & Goolkasian, P. (2010) Mindfulness meditation improves cognition: Evidence of brief mental training. *Consciousness and Cognition*, *19*, 597–605.

30. Davidson, R. J., Kabat-Zinn, J., Schumacher, J., Rosenkranz, M., Muller, D., Santorelli, S. F., ... & Sheridan, J. F. (2003). Alterations in brain and immune function produced by mindfulness meditation. *Psychosomatic Medicine*, *4*, 564–570; Ma, S. H., & Teasdale, J. D. (2004). Mindfulness-based cognitive therapy for depression: Replication and exploration of differential relapse prevention effects. *Journal of Clinical and Consulting Psychology, 72*, 31–40; Shapiro, S. L., & Brown, K. W. (2007). *The relation of mindfulness enhancement to increases in empathy in a mindfulness-based stress reduction program.* Unpublished data, Santa Clara University; Ostafin, B. D., & Marlatt, G. A. (2008). Surfing the urge: Experiential acceptance moderates the relation between automatic alcohol motivation and hazardous drinking. *Journal of Social and Clinical Psychology, 27*, 404–418; Chiesa, A., & Serreti, A. (2009). Mindfulness-based stress reduction for stress management in healthy people: A review and meta-analysis. *Journal of Alternative and Complementary Medicine, 15*, 593–600.

31. Napoli, M., Krech, P. R., & Holley, L. C. (2005). Mindfulness training for elementary school students: The Attention Academy. *Journal of Applied School Psychology, 21*, 99–125; Zylowska, L., Ackerman, D. L., Yang, M. H., Futrell, J. L., Horton, N. L., Hale, T. S., Pataki, C., & Smalley, S. L. (2008). Mindfulness meditation training in adults and adolescents with ADHD: A feasibility study. *Journal of Attention Disorders, 11*, 737–746; Beauchemin, J., Hutchins, T. L., & Patterson, F. (2008). Mindfulness meditation may lessen anxiety, promote social skills and improve academic performance among adolescents with learning disabilities. *Complementary Health Practice Review, 13*, 34–45; Britton, W. B., Haynes, P. L., Fridel, K. W., & Bootzin, R. R. (2010). Polysomnographic and subjective profiles of sleep continuity before and after mindfulness-based cognitive therapy in partially remitted depression. *Psychosomatic Medicine, 72*, 539–548; Huppert, F. A., & Johnson, D. M. (2010). A controlled trial of mindfulness training in schools: The importance of practice for an impact on well-being. *Journal of Positive Psychology, 5*, 264–274; Biegel, G. M., Brown, K. W., Shapiro, S. L., & Schubert, C. M. (2009). Mindfulness-based stress reduction for the treatment of adolescent psychiatric outpatients: A randomized clinical trial. *Journal of Consulting and Clinical Psychology, 77*, 855–866; Bogels, S., Hoogstad, B., vanDun, L., deSchutter, S., & Restifo, K. (2008). Mindfulness training for adolescents with externalizing disorders and their parents. *Behavioural and Cognitive Psychotherapy, 36*, 193–209; Semple, R. J., Lee, J., Rosa, D., & Miller, L. F. (2010). A randomized trial of mindfulness-based cognitive therapy for children: Promoting mindful attention to enhance social-emotional resiliency in children. *Journal of Child and Family Studies, 19*, 218–229.

32. Burke, C. A. (2010). Mindfulness-based approaches with children and adolescents: A preliminary review of current research in an emerging field. *Journal of Child and Family Studies, 19*, 133–144.

33. Kabat-Zinn, J. (1990). *Full catastrophe living: Using the wisdom of your body and mind to face stress, pain, and illness.* New York, NY: Delacorte.

34. Kabat-Zinn. (1990).

35. Fredrickson, B. L., Cohn, M. A., Coffey, K. A., Pek, J., & Finkel, S. M. (2008). Open hearts build lives: Positive emotions, induced through loving-

kindness meditation, build consequential personal resources. *Journal of Personality and Social Psychology, 95*, 1045–1062.

36. Blair, C., & Diamond, A. (2008). Biological processes in prevention and intervention: The promotion of self-regulation as a means of preventing school failure. *Development and Psychopathology, 20*, 899–911.

37. Lyubomirsky, S., & Tkach, C. (2004). The consequences of dysphoric rumination. In C. Papageorgiou & A. Wells (Eds.), *Depressive rumination: Nature, theory and treatment* (pp. 21–42). Hoboken, NJ: Wiley.

38. Broderick, P. C., & Blewitt, P. (in press). *The life span: Human development for helping professionals* (4th ed.). Upper Saddle River, NJ: Pearson Education.

39. Broderick, P. C., & Metz, S. (2009). Learning to BREATHE: A pilot trial of a mindfulness curriculum for adolescents. *Advances in School Mental Health Promotion, 2*, 35–46; Metz, S., Frank, J., Reibel, D., Cantrell, T., Sanders, R., & Broderick, P. C. (2012). *The effectiveness of the Learning to BREATHE program on adolescent emotion regulation*. Manuscript submitted for publication.

40. Steinberg, L. (2010). A behavioral scientist looks at the science of adolescent brain development. *Brain and Cognition, 72*, 160–164.

PATRICIA C. BRODERICK *is professor emerita, West Chester University of Pennsylvania, and research associate with the Prevention Research Center at Pennsylvania State University.*

PATRICIA A. JENNINGS *is a research assistant professor in human development and family studies and the Prevention Research Center at Pennsylvania State University.*

Index